GO INTO
the STREETS!

The Welcoming Church
of Pope Francis

**EDITED BY THOMAS P. RAUSCH, SJ
AND RICHARD R. GAILLARDETZ**

Paulist Press
New York / Mahwah, NJ

Cover image by Paul Haring, Senior Photographer, Catholic News Service, Via della Conciliazione 44, 00193 Rome, Italy

Cover design by Tamian Wood
Book design by Lynn Else

Library of Congress Cataloging-in-Publication Data

Names: Rausch, Thomas P. editor.
Title: Go into the streets! : the welcoming church of Pope Francis / edited by
    Thomas P. Rausch, SJ and Richard R. Gaillardetz.
Description: New York : Paulist Press, 2016.
Identifiers: LCCN 2015033777 (print) | LCCN 2016001171 (ebook) | ISBN
    9780809149513 (pbk. : alk. paper) | ISBN 9781587685507 (ebook)
Subjects: LCSH: Church renewal—Catholic Church. | Francis, Pope, 1936–
Classification: LCC BX1746 .G563 2016 (print) | LCC BX1746 (ebook) | DDC
    282.09/051—dc23
LC record available at http://lccn.loc.gov/2015033777

ISBN 978-0-8091-4951-3 (paperback)
ISBN 978-1-58768-550-7 (e-book)

Published by Paulist Press
997 Macarthur Boulevard
Mahwah, New Jersey 07430

www.paulistpress.com

Printed and bound in the
United States of America

To Francis, Bishop of Rome

CONTENTS

Contents

INTRODUCTION

Thomas P. Rausch, SJ

When Jorge Mario Bergoglio came to the throne of Peter in March 2013, he was not just the first Jesuit pope but also the first pope from the Global South. As such, he is more sensitive to the multicultural and pluralistic nature of the church than some of his predecessors, more inclined to recognize the authority of local churches and their episcopal conferences, and less Eurocentric in his theology. In a reflection on the Fifth General Conference of the Latin American and Caribbean Bishops (CELAM), which took place at the Brazilian shrine of Aparecida in May 2007, he spoke of the Second Vatican Council as revealing the variety of situations and cultures in which the church is active. These include the Eastern churches, churches in India, Japan, and China, young churches in Africa, the popular Catholicism of Latin America, and significantly, what he termed an "arthritic European Christianity."[1]

His Jesuit heritage becomes evident in his strong appreciation of traditional piety (*religiosidad popular* in the Spanish), with its emphasis on feeling or sentiment. Faith, he says, is ruled by sentiments (*sentimientos*) of the heart that become expressed in thoughtful gestures toward God and one's brothers and sisters. He appeals to John of the Cross, Teresa of Avila, and Ignatius of

Loyola to show that sentiment is not incompatible with deep spiritual experience. These Spanish mystics and reformers show the affective side of faith. Francis values traditional piety because it touches the heart, entering into the daily life of the people.

Part of his concern here is to avoid the temptation to intellectualize one's faith, concentrating "only on ideas and formulations that do not result in a commitment of one's life."[2] Though some of his critics have suggested that Francis is "anti-theological," he is a complex thinker. He is allergic to ideologies, whether of the left or the right. What he wants is a concrete theological language that brings others to the gospel and to Christ. Such language is of necessity multicultural. As he says in *Evangelii gaudium*, "We cannot demand that peoples of every continent, in expressing their Christian faith, imitate modes of expression which European nations developed at a particular moment of their history, because the faith cannot be constricted to the limits of understanding and expression of any one culture" (no. 118).

Thus Pope Francis stresses the importance of the inculturation of the faith in traditional piety or popular religion. More than the faith of simple people, traditional piety is rooted in the human person's openness to the transcendent; as a synthesis of faith and culture, it is a form of theology. He argues that traditional piety in Latin America resists modernity's efforts to subordinate faith to the dictates of reason. He cites the Puebla Document (1979), which saw in Latin American traditional piety "a treasury of values that reflect Christian wisdom."[3] For those displaced from the countryside to the secular, postmodern city, traditional piety, with its devotions, saints, and fiestas, helps the stranger feel at home.

THE JESUIT

The story of Pope Francis has not been without controversy. There are two narratives. During the difficult years of the Argentinian "Dirty War" (1974–83), many Jesuits saw Bergoglio's leadership style as authoritarian during his tenure as a very young provincial of the Argentine province (1973–79) and later as rector of the Jesuit Colegio Máximo of philosophy and theology at San Miguel (1980–86). But others, particularly the young, saw him as a charismatic leader. Fearing he was a divisive force in the province, a new provincial in 1986 sent him to Germany for a "sabbatical." Returning to Argentina after seven months, he taught a course at the Máximo and wrote on spirituality. In 1990, he was removed from the course and sent into quasi-exile in Córdova, miles from Buenos Aires. Later, he described this experience as "a time of great interior crisis."

According to Paul Vallely, Bergoglio experienced a profound conversion while in Córdova, returning "an utterly different man." When he took up his new job as an auxiliary bishop in Buenos Aires in 1992, "the old Bergoglio had vanished." In his place was a bishop with a new model of leadership, "one which involved listening, participation and collegiality." Soon the formerly authoritarian superior was being called the Bishop of the Slums.[4]

However, Austen Ivereigh paints a different picture of Bergoglio, describing him as a strong leader and reformer both as provincial and rector. In Ivereigh's account, much of the opposition came from a group of Jesuits at the Center for Social Research and Action (CIAS), older academics using the social sciences to analyze social injustice. To them, Bergoglio lacked the requisite academic credentials. They were also uncomfortable with his "conservative" emphasis on popular religion, sometimes identified with the *teología del pueblo*, an Argentine version of liberation theology without the elements of Enlightenment liberalism or Marxism that Bergoglio dismissed as ideology. They saw him as attacking the symptoms of poverty but not its root causes and as rejecting their progressive model of Jesuit renewal for his own notion of Ignatian and Jesuit identity. Instead, Bergoglio stressed the inculturation of the faith, and direct contact with the poor. While rector, he started a farm at the college to give the scholastics, largely from middle-class backgrounds, a taste of the lives of the poor as well as to help feed those in the neighborhood. As Ivereigh comments, "It is striking how often the criticism of Bergoglio was expressed in enlightenment terms of progress-regress."[5]

There is probably truth in both accounts. In his famous interview with Father Antonio Spadaro, Francis acknowledged that his authoritarian style of government and quick manner of making decisions had many faults: "I did not always do the necessary consultation. And this was not a good thing." But, he adds that he has never been a "right-winger."[6] The fact that his province sent him to the Thirty-third General Congregation in 1983 and elected him as procurator in 1987 shows that he continued to be held in high regard.

BISHOP BERGOGLIO

The new Bishop Bergoglio continued his direct service of the poor. He wandered the *villas miserias* and spent long hours talking with the people, blessing their children, pausing to drink maté with them (maté is a strong caffeinated Argentinian drink), and visiting their homes. He helped the *cartoneros*—desperately poor people in Buenos Aires who at night sorted through the city's garbage in search of recyclable materials and things to sell—to form a union. He supported self-help groups, political organizations, and cooperatives, and began to speak of oppressive economic systems as "structures of sin," denouncing "the unjust distribution of goods." Always, his approach was pastoral, to help those in need.

Some bishops found him too progressive, too involved with the poor, and thus divisive. Others increasingly recognized him as a leader. Bergoglio was made Archbishop of Buenos Aires in 1998, remaining as controversial as before. Pope John Paul II named him cardinal in 2001. In 2007, at the Fifth General Conference of the Latin American and Caribbean Bishops (CELAM) at Aparecida, he was elected to chair the important committee charged with drafting the final document. "One detail confirms his popularity: on the day he celebrated Mass in the Sanctuary of Aparecida, the people applauded at the end of his homily, the only time that something like that ever happened."[7]

In an interview given shortly after CELAM concluded, Cardinal Bergoglio called its final document "an act of the Magisterium of the Latin American church," stressing its representative character. "It's perhaps the first time that one of our General Conferences didn't start out from a pre-prepared basic text but from open dialogue, that had already begun earlier between the CELAM and the Episcopal Conferences, and that has since continued....Our stance was that of receiving everything that came from below, from the People of God, and to make not so much a synthesis, as a harmony." He went on to speak of the importance of celebrating Mass with the thousands of pilgrims and believers at the shrine. "Celebrating the Eucharist together with the people is different from celebrating it amongst us bishops separately. That gave us a live sense of belonging to our people, of the Church that goes forward as People of God, of us bishops as its servants."[8]

POPE FRANCIS

Central to Pope Francis's understanding of his mission is a reform of the Curia as well as reclaiming the Second Vatican Council's collegial vision of the church as a communion of the faithful with their pastors. He sees the Council as representing an opportunity to dialogue with the contemporary world, meaning both "a certain reconciliation with the enlightened modernity and the recovery of a prophetic dimension of the Church in society."[9] Nowhere is this more apparent than in his 2015 encyclical *Laudato si'* on what he calls "our Sister, Mother Earth" (no. 2), using the language of Saint Francis. Addressed to every person living on the planet, thus other churches and Christian communities, other religions, all people of good will, it wants to draw on the best scientific research available to us today (no. 15). Acknowledging that the church does not have all the answers, it calls repeatedly for dialogue (no. 61).

How that dialogue will unfold is only beginning to become clear, but Pope Francis, who insists that reality is more important than ideas, has already given signs that he expects something different from what has been Rome's cautious, hierarchical approach to pastoral problems in the church's life. In this book, we will explore his understanding of church.

In chapter 1, Robert Imbelli traces the theological continuity between Popes Benedict XVI and Francis, despite differences in their personal gifts, styles, and pastoral sensitivities. Both were profoundly influenced by the *ressourcement* theologian and later Cardinal Henri de Lubac. Both shared his emphasis on encountering the living person of Jesus, on beauty as a way of joining the human heart with the Divine, and on the profound connection between the risen Christ, the Eucharist, and the church. Both also stress the essentially communal and social nature of Catholicism.

The next two chapters provide some deep background of Bergoglio. Writing from a Latin American perspective in chapter 2, Maria Clara Bingemer traces the emergence of liberation theology in the years after the Second Vatican Council, as well as the efforts of the Latin American bishops to interpret the Bible in a transformative way, especially for those living at the margins. Important for understanding Pope Francis is the uniquely Argentinian version of liberation theology, the *teología del pueblo* or "theology of the people." She also reviews Bergoglio's work with the *curas villeros*, the priests who minister in the *villas miserias* of Buenos Aires.

Drawing on Bergoglio's earlier writings, Cecilia González-Andrieu unpacks Francis's understanding of the often underappreciated "popular religion" (*religiosidad popular*) in chapter 3, showing how it embraces a multiplicity of cultural strands expressive of a people's experience of the Divine. Particularly important is its capacity to incorporate the poor into the church's life and worship, while Francis's appreciation of the affective and the aesthetic dimensions of the gospel reveals beauty as a way to God.

In chapter 4, Gerard Mannion examines Francis's efforts to reclaim the vision of Pope John XXIII and the Second Vatican Council. Using the pope's apostolic exhortation, *Evangelii gaudium*, he unpacks the pope's commitment to a more collegial style of governance throughout the church. Francis wants to reclaim the image of the church as the people of God and to reengage the laity, challenging them to become missionary disciples, giving them voice, and encouraging dialogue.

Thomas Rausch, in chapter 5, explores Francis's concern for an official church that consults and listens. Key themes include his take on Ignatius of Loyola's principle of "thinking with the church," which for Francis means the *whole* church, not just the hierarchy, the church's *infallibilitas in credendo* and its relation to the *sensus fidei* that sees the whole church as believing subject. The sometimes contentious debates at the 2014 Extraordinary Assembly of the Synod of Bishops on the Family suggest what a listening church might look like.

Grounding Francis's emphasis on dialogue in Pope Paul VI's encyclical, *Ecclesiam suam*, Catherine Clifford in chapter 6 looks at dialogue as a self-critical process in which the Church reexamines the gap between its self-understanding and its actual life. That means challenging the Church to reconsider its attitudes, structures, and practices, and encouraging the lay faithful to contribute to that process. Clifford shows how Francis wants to see dialogue in social, ecumenical, and interreligious areas.

In chapter 7, Christopher Ruddy explores Francis's efforts to reconfigure the relationship between the universal church and the local churches, focusing not on documents but on his language and gestures. Thus, he says "Bishop of Rome" rather than pope, has revised where a new archbishop receives his pallium, chose the majority of his cardinals not from the Roman Curia but from the various continents, and cited frequently in his apostolic exhortation, *Evangelii gaudium,* documents from national and regional episcopal conferences around the world. Ruddy argues that for Francis, the church's center is to be found in its peripheries.

In chapter 8, Richard Gaillardetz develops Francis's understanding of the pastoral orientation of doctrine. Without necessarily revising official teaching, like John XXIII, Francis consistently recontextualizes these teachings in the service of the church's pastoral mission, even as he also remains open to the possibility that a particular doctrine may need to be reformulated. Important here is the neglected principle of the "hierarchy of truths" as well as the pope's emphasis on the "medicine of mercy."

Richard Lennan's chapter 9 builds on the pope's metaphors of the church as a community of missionary disciples and as a "field hospital" in a wounded world. With an overview of the development of the concept of ministry in recent Catholic thought, he suggests that changes in the church's ordained ministry and the emergence of new forms of ministry place new challenges before the church. Again, from the perspective of mercy, Lennan develops the pope's description of ministers as doorkeepers ("ostiaries") and reviews his concerns regarding the ministry of priests today.

In chapter 10, Christine Firer Hinze grounds Francis's approach to social justice in earlier papal encyclicals and episcopal documents, especially those of the General Conference of the Latin American bishops (CELAM). She focuses on several key themes in Catholic social teaching and on the pope's unique approach, especially his emphasis on justice as God's mercy. Finally, she examines what she calls three "base-points" of the church's social mission.

The new energy that Pope Francis has brought to his ministry as Bishop of Rome, often referred to as the "Francis effect," has called forth an enthusiastic response from both Catholics and non-Catholics. It is the hope of the authors of this study that his efforts to shape a more welcoming church, bringing it "into the streets" and to those on the peripheries, may help it more fully image God's love and mercy, revealed in the person of Jesus.

NOTES

1. Jorge Mario Bergoglio, "Religiosidad Popular Como Inculturación de la Fe," in *Testigos de Aparecida*, vol. 2 (Bogota: CELAM, 2009), 281–325; English translation, "Traditional Piety as Inculturation of the Faith," in *Family and Life: Pastoral Reflections*, trans. James Crowley (Mahwah, NJ: Paulist Press, 2015), 75.

2. Ibid., 308–14, at 313.

3. Documento de Puebla III Conferencia General del Episcopado Latinoamericano, La religiosidad del pueblo, en su núcleo, es un acervo de valores que responde con sabiduría Cristiana, no. 448.

4. Paul Vallely, "The Crisis that Changed Pope Francis," *Newsweek*, October 23, 2014; http://www.newsweek.com/2014/10/31/crisis-changed-pope-francis-279303.html; see also his *Pope Francis: Untying the Knots* (London: Bloomsbury, 2013), 37–61.

5. Austen Ivereigh, *The Great Reformer: Francis and the Making of a Radical Pope* (New York: Henry Holt and Company, 2014) 188–204, at 193; Ivereigh identifies three priests, Lucio Gera, Rafael Tello, and the Jesuit Juan Carlos Scannone with the teología del pueblo, 111.

6. Pope Francis, "A Big Heart Open to God: The Exclusive Interview with Pope Francis," *America* 209, no. 8 (September 30, 2013): 20; http://www.americamagazine.org/pope-interview.

7. Ernesto Cavassa, "On the Trail of Aparacida," *America*, October 31, 2013, http://americamagazine.org/trail-aparecida.

8. "What I Would Have Said at the Consistory," Interview with Cardinal Jorge Mario Bergoglio by Sefania Falasca, *30 Days* 11 (2007); http://www.30giorni.it/articoli_id_16457_ l3.htm.

9. Bergoglio, "Religiosidad Popular Como Inculturación de la Fe," 287; translation by James Crowley.

CHAPTER 1

BENEDICT AND FRANCIS

Robert P. Imbelli

INTRODUCTION

To have heard Pope Emeritus Benedict preach in Saint Peter's Basilica was to have experienced a wonderfully crafted homily, read in fluent Italian, though occasionally flavored with a German accent. To see Pope Francis preach in the same church is to see animated gestures, reinforcing the words. Not infrequently, the words themselves are improvised as Francis interacts with the congregation, an occasional Spanish expression spicing the exchange. However, the commonality of their ecclesiological vision unites them more intimately than the unmistakable differences of spiritual gifts, personal style, and pastoral sensitivities.[1]

Austen Ivereigh, in his fine biography of Francis, stresses this theological continuity between Benedict and Francis. He suggestively compares their theological affinity to the relation between Saint Benedict of Nursia and Saint Francis of Assisi. Francis of Assisi drew upon the riches of the Benedictine tradition to promote a new style of evangelization in the new world of the High Middle Ages. The open-door hospitality of the Benedictine monastery (from which Saint Francis often benefitted) no longer sufficed; it was necessary to go into the newly emerging cities to proclaim the gospel to the multitudes. Now, apropos our last two popes, Ivereigh writes, "Another Francis was taking Benedict on the road."[2]

THE DE LUBAC CONNECTION

Whether on the desk in Benedict's study or in the battered briefcase Francis carries with him on his journeys, one author has pride of place in their appropriation of a Catholic ecclesiology: the distinguished Jesuit theologian and later Cardinal Henri de Lubac. Two of de Lubac's books, in particular, have formed their ecclesial vision. *Catholicism*, originally written in 1938, promoted the "ressourcement," the return to Scripture, liturgy, and the fathers of the Church, that was to come to full flower at the Second Vatican Council.[3] Two features of the book were to provide compelling contributions to the renewal of Catholic ecclesiology and to the ecclesial visions of Ratzinger and Bergoglio. The first was the recovery of a sense of the Church as "mystery" or "sacrament," deeper than its always necessary institutional embodiment. The second was a recovery of the "social" and "communal" nature of the Church, in the face of a reduction of the gospel and the Church's mission to a question of the salvation of the individual.

The second book, written in 1953, after de Lubac had been removed from his teaching position, was his love song celebrating the spouse of Jesus Christ: *Méditation sur l'église.*[4] Noteworthy in the book are profound mediations upon the "Mystery of the Church," the Church as "Sacrament of Jesus Christ," "Church as Mother," and "Temptations with regard to the Church"—all chapter titles within the book. These themes inspired Vatican II's great Constitution on the Church: *Lumen gentium.* They also found their way into the hearts of Joseph Ratzinger and Jorge Mario Bergoglio.

MYSTICISM NOT MORALISM

In the chapter of *Méditation*, significantly titled "*Ecclesia Mater*" (Mother Church), de Lubac sketches a striking portrait of the person who is being nourished by the Church's sacramental life. Foremost among the qualities of such a person is this: he or she "will take great care not to allow, little by little, some generic idea to take the place of the Person of Jesus Christ."[5] Throughout the chapter, de Lubac shows his deep appreciation of the importance of the Church's dogmatic tradition. However, he is equally alert to the danger of its becoming hardened and thus losing its essential "mystagogical" quality. Dogma is meant to point to, not replace, the living Person, Jesus Christ.

It is this same sensitivity that leads Benedict XVI to write in his inaugural encyclical, *Deus caritas est*, the much-quoted affirmation: "Being Christian is not the result of an ethical choice or a lofty idea, but the encounter with an event, a person, which gives life a new horizon and a decisive direction" (no. 1).[6] Significantly, Pope Francis quotes these very words at the beginning of his missionary manifesto, the apostolic exhortation *Evangelii gaudium* (EG). And Francis introduces them by writing, "I never tire of repeating those words of Benedict XVI which take us to the very heart of the Gospel" (no. 7).[7]

Neither for Benedict nor Francis does this emphasis at all imply an unconcern for distinctive Christian dispositions and actions. Yet, their primary concern is to show how these actions proceed from a genuine personal encounter with Jesus Christ. Moreover, this Person is not some figure from a remote past, but the risen Lord acting in the Church. In a memorable homily preached on the Solemnity of Mary, Mother of God, Pope Francis proclaimed,

> Our faith is not an abstract doctrine or philosophy, but a vital and full relationship with a person: Jesus Christ, the only-begotten Son of God who became man, was put to death, rose from the dead to save us, and is now living in our midst. Where can we encounter him? We encounter him in the Church, in our hierarchical, Holy Mother Church. It is the Church which says today:

13

"Behold the Lamb of God"; it is the Church, which proclaims him; it is in the Church that Jesus continues to
accomplish his acts of grace which are the sacraments.[8]

To which words, Benedict XVI would utter a rousing "Amen!"

Another sensibility shared between Benedict and Francis is a
recognition of the surpassing importance, in presenting and
appropriating Christian faith, of what Francis calls the *"via pul-
chritudinis"*—the way of beauty. He writes of the need for "a
renewed esteem for beauty as a means of touching the human
heart and enabling the truth and goodness of the Risen Christ to
radiate within it" (EG 167).

Benedict XVI often expressed a similar conviction concerning the crucial importance of images in touching the human heart
and fostering a personal relation with the Lord. A salient example
of his commitment to "the way of beauty" was his incorporation
of fifteen color prints as integral elements in the *Compendium of
the Catechism of the Catholic Church*. He wrote in justification of
their inclusion: "Today more than ever, in a culture of images, a
sacred image can express much more than what can be said in
words, and be an extremely effective and dynamic way of communicating the Gospel message."[9]

Neither for Benedict nor Francis does an appreciation and
promotion of the aesthetic signal mere aestheticism. The way of
beauty is inseparable from the way of truth: the confession of
Jesus Christ whose death and resurrection constitutes him Lord
of the Church and Redeemer of the world. As Francis declared in
his very first homily to the cardinals after his election as pope,
"My wish is that all of us, after these days of grace, will have the
courage, yes, the courage, to walk in the presence of the Lord, with
the Lord's Cross; to build the Church on the Lord's blood which
was poured out on the Cross; and to profess the one glory: Christ
crucified." Without Christ at the center, the Church becomes only
a "charitable NGO [nongovernmental organization]!"[10] It is the
personal and experiential relation with the living Lord, Jesus

Christ, that places mysticism, not moralism as the heart of the Church's life.[11]

THE BODY AND ITS HEAD

One of Henri de Lubac's outstanding contributions to twentieth-century Catholic ecclesiology was to recover the early Church's sense of the profound interconnection among the risen Christ, the Eucharist, and the Church. He refers to the "tri-form body of Christ" to express the organic relationship among these foundational realities of faith. Thus he writes in *Méditation sur l'église*,

> The Head and the members form one single body. The Bridegroom and the Bride are but "one flesh." There are not two Christs, of which one is personal and the other "mystical." Of course, the Head and the members are not to be confused; and Christians are not the physical (or "Eucharistic") body of Christ. The Bride is not herself the Bridegroom. All the distinctions remain; but there is no discontinuity. Moreover, the Church is not just any body: she is the body of Christ.[12]

This acute sense of the intimate and inseparable relation between Christ and the Church permeates the writings and homilies of both Benedict and Francis.

One hears explicit echoes of de Lubac in Benedict XVI's apostolic exhortation *Sacramentum caritatis*, which he wrote subsequent to the 2005 Synod of Bishops devoted to the Eucharist. Benedict teaches, "Christian antiquity used the same words, *Corpus Christi*, to designate Christ's body born of the Virgin Mary, his Eucharistic body, and his ecclesial body. This clear datum of the tradition helps us to appreciate the inseparability of Christ and the Church."[13] At the same time, though the relation between Christ and the Church is intimate, it is not proportionate. Christ remains the Head upon which the Church is dependent for its very life. As Benedict says, "The Eucharist is Christ who gives himself to us and continually builds us up as his body...the Church's ability to [celebrate] the Eucharist is completely rooted in Christ's self-gift to her."[14]

Pope Francis has delivered two sets of catecheses on Church at his Wednesday audiences. In each of them, he has dwelt on the topic of the Church as the body of Christ. Here is one way he expresses the intimacy of the relation of Christ and the Church:

> The Church is not a welfare, cultural or political association but a living body that walks and acts in history. And this body has a head, Jesus, who guides, feeds and supports it. This is a point that I would like to emphasize: if one separates the head from the rest of the body, the whole person cannot survive. It is like this in the Church: we must stay ever more deeply connected with Jesus. But not only that: just as it is important that life blood flow through the body in order to live, so must we allow Jesus to work in us, let his Word guide us, his presence in the Eucharist feed us, give us life, his love strengthen our love for our neighbor.[15]

As is clear from the above quotes, both Francis and Benedict show great sensitivity to Christ's eucharistic nourishing of his body, the Church. But Francis develops this insight in a distinctive way. He speaks often about the Church as "mother" who gives birth to those being redeemed in Christ and to the Eucharist, not as gift to the worthy, but as "medicine of mercy."

In his two sets of catecheses on Church, he significantly devotes two sessions in each to the theme of Church as Mother. In the audience of September 11, 2013, he admitted, "For me it is one of the most beautiful images of Church: Mother Church."[16] A number of elements contribute to the power of this image for Francis. First, it underscores that the Church births believers in the new supernatural life that comes from God. Second, it stresses that within the Church, believers are continually nourished in that life through the sacraments and the preaching of the Word. Third, it leads to the realization that, having received life from Mother Church, we are not left passive, but are called to participate actively in the Church's maternal function by our generous sharing of faith and life with others. Thus he concludes his catechesis with typical Franciscan flair:

> The Church is all of us: from the baby just baptized to the Bishop, the Pope; we are all the Church and we are all equal in the eyes of God! We are all called to collaborate for the birth of new Christians in the faith, we are all called to be educators in the faith, to proclaim the Gospel. Each of us should ask our self: what do I do so that others might share in Christian life? Am I generous in my faith or am I closed? When I repeat that I love a Church that is not closed in herself, but capable of coming out, of moving, even with risks, to bring Christ to all people, I am thinking of everyone, of me, of you, of every Christian! We all take part in the motherhood of the church, so that the light of Christ may reach the far confines of the earth. Long live Holy Mother Church!

It should be clear that the image of Church as Mother does not replace, for Francis, but, rather, mediates the life whose source is the risen Christ, the Head of the Church. For, as the title of *Lumen gentium* makes abundantly clear, Christ alone is the Light of the World. As with Benedict, so with Francis: the ecclesiology of both is foundationally Christocentric. Indeed, in his remarkable preconclave address to the meetings of the Cardinals, Bergoglio spoke of the *mysterium lunae*. The only mission of the Church is to be like the moon: reflecting the greater light, the Light who is Christ. But, then, he invoked de Lubac to lament that when the Church becomes centered on itself, ceasing to reflect Christ, it succumbs to that spiritual worldliness that is its mortal danger.[17]

17

"NO TO SPIRITUAL WORLDLINESS"

In *The Great Reformer*, Ivereigh speaks in dramatic language of the influence of de Lubac's *Méditation sur l'église* upon Jorge Mario Bergoglio. He states that Bergoglio was "haunted by the final pages" of the book.[18] He is referring to the last chapter, titled "The Church and the Virgin Mary," where de Lubac, in the book's very last pages, introduces the term *spiritual worldliness*. The term has become a hallmark of Bergoglio's discernment as spiritual director, provincial, and pope. Indeed, it appears as the title of a crucial section of *Evangelii gaudium*. Here is how Francis himself sums up the peril: "Spiritual worldliness, which hides behind piety and even love for the Church, consists in seeking not the Lord's glory, but human glory and personal well being." Francis warns that were it to infiltrate into the Church (he then quotes de Lubac directly), "it would be infinitely more disastrous than all purely moral worldliness" (EG 93).

Francis goes on to identify two forms of such spiritual worldliness—temptations—that beset, one might say, the Catholic "right" and "left." What they have in common is that neither is "really concerned about Jesus Christ or others." Both are "manifestations of an anthropocentric humanism" that belies the Church's unique vocation to engender in human beings, through Christ, the new life of the Spirit. Francis concludes, starkly but realistically, "It is impossible to think that a genuine evangelizing thrust could emerge from these adulterated forms of Christianity" (EG 94).

In this vein, one should note Pope Francis's important Address to the Leadership of the Episcopal Conference of Latin America (CELAM) during his 2013 Journey to Brazil for World Youth Day. There he dwelt on "Some Temptations against Missionary Discipleship" that reduce the gospel to an ideology. Some on the left presume to be an elite, ushering the masses into a utopian future detached from the concrete demands of the gospel; others on the right seek refuge in an idealized past, refusing to discern the signs of the times in the light of the gospel. In their place, Francis proposes the salient characteristic of the "missionary disciple"—he or she "is a self-transcending subject, a subject projected towards encounter: an encounter with the Master (who anoints us as his disciples) and an encounter with men and women who await the message."[19]

Within this context of a decided "no" to spiritual worldliness, Francis's "Christmas Address" to the Roman Curia takes on its full spiritual and ecclesial import. Recall that the pope enumerates fifteen "spiritual diseases or temptations" that afflict those called to serve the church in the ranks of its central administration. It is significant that, in offering his spiritual discernment, he draws upon the ecclesiology of the church as the Body of Christ (even referring explicitly to Pius XII's pioneering encyclical *Mystici corporis*). The root of the spiritual ailment for the members of the Curia, as for all the members of Christ's ecclesial body, is the failure to remain united with its Head, to be continually nourished by Christ in the new life he offers. He says, "The Curia, like the Church, cannot live without a vital, personal, authentic, and solid relationship with Christ." And he concludes with an appeal to the mystical heart of the Christian life: "And so we are called—in this Christmas season and throughout our time of service and our lives—to live 'in truth and love, [growing] in every way into him who is the head, into Christ, from whom the whole body, joined and knit together by every ligament with which it is equipped, as each part is working properly, promotes the body's growth in building itself up in love (Eph 4:15–16).'"[20]

Though Francis provides a fuller checklist in his frequent calls for a serious examination of conscience on the part of all the followers of Christ, Benedict XVI did not ignore the manifold infidelities that disfigure the Body of Christ. During the Good Friday Way of the Cross, shortly before his election as pope, Cardinal Ratzinger decried the "filth" in the church, "even among those who, in the priesthood, ought to belong entirely to him."[21] And in his last apostolic voyage to his native Germany, Benedict spoke words that were not always welcomed by the financially wealthy

German church. He said, "History has shown that, when the Church becomes less worldly, her missionary witness shines more brightly. Once liberated from material and political burdens and privileges, the Church can reach out more effectively and in a truly Christian way to the whole world, she can be truly open to the world."[22]

Liberated from spiritual worldliness—a never-ending challenge—the church can truly embark upon its constitutive missionary task, giving itself fully to the new evangelization. Benedict told his hearers, "It is not a question here of finding a new strategy to re-launch the Church. Rather, it is a question of setting aside mere strategy and seeking total transparency, not bracketing or ignoring anything from the truth of our present situation, but living the faith fully here and now in the utterly sober light of day, appropriating it completely, and stripping away from it anything that only seems to belong to faith, but in truth is mere convention or habit."[23]

Both Benedict and Francis are convinced with de Lubac of the transcendent newness and the surpassing joy of the gospel. As de Lubac had written, "The Lord's Resurrection has created a new world; it marks the beginning of a new age; it has founded on earth a type of existence that is absolutely new."[24] That conviction receives dramatic expression in *Evangelii gaudium* when Francis quotes Saint Irenaeus: "By his coming, Christ brought all newness in himself." Then Francis continues, "With his newness Christ is always able to renew our life and our community" (no. 11). Spiritual worldliness is the refusal to live the new life that Christ, through his life, death, and resurrection has revealed and enabled. It is the refusal to put Christ at the center of our lives, and to prefer that we ourselves be the center.[25] It is the refusal to live as a member of Christ's body. And the poisoned fruit is the corruption of the church's mission. As de Lubac trenchantly laments—a lament in which both Benedict and Francis join: "How can the world believe in the Bridegroom, if, in our lives, the Bride appears barren?"[26]

SOLIDARITY

An underappreciated but central aspect of Benedict XVI's ecclesiology is its intrinsically communal nature. He early learned from de Lubac the intrinsically "social" dimension of Catholicism.[27] In speaking of the Eucharist, Joseph Ratzinger articulates the newness of life in Christ in these words:

> The Eucharist is never an event involving just two, a dialogue between Christ and me. Eucharistic communion is aimed at a complete reshaping of my own life. It breaks up man's entire self and creates a new "we." Communion with Christ is necessarily also communication with all who belong to him. Thereby I myself become part of the new bread he is creating by the resubstantiation of the whole of earthly reality.[28]

He repeats this insistence in his first encyclical as pope, *Deus caritas est*. There he writes, "Union with Christ is also union with all those to whom he gives himself. I cannot possess Christ just for myself. I can belong to him only in union with all those who have become, or will become, his own" (no. 14).[29]

Perhaps Benedict's most striking affirmation of the solidarity that unites all people in Christ (whether they know him by name or not) may be found in the great encyclical on hope: *Spe salvi*. There Benedict writes,

> Our hope is always essentially also hope for others; only thus is it truly hope for me too. As Christians we should never limit ourselves to asking: how can I save myself? We should also ask: what can I do in order that others may be saved and that for them too the star of hope may rise? Then I will have done my utmost for my own personal salvation as well. (no. 48)[30]

The theme of solidarity permeates the theology of Pope Francis as well. In the interview with Antonio Spadaro, Francis confesses that "the image of the Church I like is that of the holy, faithful people of God….In the history of salvation God has saved a people…no one is saved alone."[31] But then he strongly denies that he is advocating "a form of populism;" for he is speaking of "the experience of holy mother the hierarchical church, as St. Ignatius called it, the Church as the people of God, pastors and people together."[32]

In his catecheses on church, Francis sounds a number of themes that are central to his understanding of the term. He insists that one becomes a member of the people of God not by physical birth, but by rebirth in the Spirit of Jesus Christ. Further, the new "law" of this people is the law of Christ: the unbounded love of God and of neighbor. This is the "law" incumbent upon the whole people of God. Finally, the people of God has a universal mission in the world. Francis declares, with passion, "What is this people's mission? It is to bring the hope and salvation of God to the world: to be a sign of the love of God who calls everyone to friendship with Him; to be the leaven that makes the dough rise, the salt that gives flavor and preserves from corruption, to be a light that enlightens."[33]

It is known that Joseph Ratzinger expressed misgivings about the use of the term *people of God* in certain circles after the Council. He discerned evidence of a "sociological and political reduction" of the term, neglecting its defining characteristic as the people whose life and vocation depended solely upon God.[34] Francis makes it clear in *Evangelii gaudium* that his use of the term is primarily theological. After all, it is God's "holy people" that is responsive to *Lumen gentium*'s "universal call to holiness." And it is God's "faithful people" whose devotion often receives expression in the "popular piety" of the church in Latin America. This popular piety, especially in terms of Marian devotion, clearly provides rich nourishment for Francis's own life of faith.

Hence there is no opposition between the two images of church as "people of God" and "Body of Christ." For both derive from the realization of the inexhaustible "Mystery of the Church": the title of both the first chapter of de Lubac's *Méditation sur l'église* and of the Second Vatican Council's Constitution on the church. Joseph Ratzinger indicates their profound interconnection when he writes, "The Church is the people of God which lives on the Body of Christ and which itself becomes the body of Christ in the celebration of the Eucharist."[35] And Ratzinger would have nothing but approbation for Francis's words in his catechesis:

> [T]he Church is the Body of Christ! And this is not simply a catchphrase: indeed, we truly are! It is the great gift that we receive on the day of our Baptism! In the sacrament of Baptism, indeed, Christ makes us his, welcoming us into the heart of the mystery of the Cross, the supreme mystery of his love for us, in order to cause us to then be raised with him, as new beings. See: in this way the Church is born, and in this way the Church is recognized as the Body of Christ! Baptism constitutes a true rebirth, which regenerates us in Christ, renders us a part of Him, and unites us intimately among ourselves, as limbs of the same body, of which He is the Head.[36]

MOBILIZING FOR MISSION

We began our exploration of the ecclesial visions of Benedict XVI and Francis underlining, with Austin Ivereigh, the theological affinity between the two pontiffs. This is certainly not to deny differences. Perhaps the primary one is picturesquely caught by Ivereigh in his quip that Francis is taking Benedict "on the road." *Evangelii gaudium* lays out the road map for the journey. Francis is striving to "put all things in a missionary key" (EG 34). And he admits to dreaming of a missionary imperative: one that is "capable of transforming everything, so that the Church's customs, ways of doing things, times and schedules, language and structures can be suitably channeled for the evangelization of today's world rather than for her self-preservation" (EG 27).

It is not that Benedict was unconcerned with the imperative of mission. Indeed, he gave considerable emphasis to the new evangelization. But with Francis, it takes on a new urgency and is directed in a special way to the "peripheries" of society, to the poor and marginalized. Francis is marshaling the resources of the church, in an unparalleled way, toward this end. It is a work of passionate love. As Francis writes, "The primary reason for evangelizing is the love of Jesus which we have received, the experience of salvation which urges us to ever greater love of him. What kind of love would not feel the need to speak of the beloved, to point him out, to make him known?" (EG 264).

What intimately supports and sustains the ecclesial vision of Benedict and Francis is this conviction: if the center who is Jesus Christ is secure, one can venture courageously to the farthest peripheries without losing the Way.[37]

NOTES

1. The present essay particularly stresses the Christological foundation of the ecclesiology of both Benedict and Francis. Some of the differences that characterize the approach of each will appear in the following essays.

2. Austen Ivereigh, *The Great Reformer: The Making of a Radical Pope* (New York: Henry Holt, 2014), 89.

3. Henri de Lubac, *Catholicism: Christ and the Common Destiny of Man*, trans. Lancelot C. Sheppard and Sister Elizabeth Englund, OCD (San Francisco: Ignatius Press, 1988). Note: this edition has a foreword by then Cardinal Ratzinger in which he speaks of the book, which he first read in 1949, as "an essential milestone of my theological journey."

4. Henri de Lubac, *Méditation sur l'église* (Paris: Aubier, 1953). The title of the English translation, *The Splendor of the Church* (San Francisco: Ignatius Press, 1953), lends a somewhat misleading "triumphalist" tone. For the influence of de Lubac's work on Francis, see Antonio Spadaro's now famous "Conversation with

Pope Francis," published as *A Big Heart Open to God* (New York: HarperCollins, 2013), 5. See also under "Lubac" in the index to Ivereigh, *The Great Reformer*, 437.

5. de Lubac, *Méditation*, 217: my translation; see *Splendor*, 250.

6. See http://w2.vatican.va/content/benedict-xvi/en/encycli cals/documents/hf_ben-xvi_enc_20051225_deus-caritas-est.html.

7. See http://w2.vatican.va/content/francesco/en/apost_ exhortations/documents/papa-francesco_esortazione-ap_20131 124_evangelii-gaudium.html.

8. Francis, "Homily for the Solemnity of Mary, Mother of God," January 1, 2015, http://w2.vatican.va/content/francesco /en/homilies/2015/documents/papa-francesco_20150101_ omelia-giornata-mondiale-pace.html.

9. *Compendium: Catechism of the Catholic Church* (Washington, DC: United States Conference of Catholic Bishops, 2006), xvii.

10. Francis, "Homily to the Cardinal Electors: March 14, 2013," http://w2.vatican.va/content/francesco/en/homilies/2013 /documents/papa-francesco_20130314_omelia-cardinali.html.

11. See Spadaro, *A Big Heart Open to God*, where Francis says, "I am rather close to the mystical movement" within the Society of Jesus and declares that Peter Faber (a model for Francis whom he canonized in the first year of his pontificate) "was a mystic," 21.

12. de Lubac, *Méditation*, 135: my translation; see *Splendor*, 158.

13. Benedict XVI, *The Sacrament of Charity* (Washington, DC: United States Conference of Catholic Bishops, 2007), 15.

14. Ibid., 14.

15. Francis, "Audience of June 19, 2013," http://w2.vatican. va/content/francesco/en/audiences/2013/documents/papa-francesco_20130619_udienza-generale.html.

16. Francis, "Audience of September 11, 2013," http://w2. vatican.va/content/francesco/en/audiences/2013/documents/pap a-francesco_20130911_udienza-generale.html.

17. See the account of the speech in Ivereigh, *The Great Reformer*, 357–59.

18. Ibid., 241.

19. Francis, "Address to the Leadership of the Episcopal Conferences of Latin America," http://w2.vatican.va/content/francesco/en/speeches/2013/july/documents/papa-francesco_20130728_gmg-celam-rio.html.

20. Francis, "Christmas Address to the Roman Curia," http://w2.vatican.va/content/francesco/en/speeches/2014/december/documents/papa-francesco_20141222_curia-romana.html.

21. See the report, http://www.catholicnews.com/services/englishnews/2010/pope-s-way-of-the-cross-2010-service-focuses-on-essentials-of-faith.cfm.

22. Benedict XVI, "It Is Time for the Church to Set Aside Her Worldliness," Freiburg, Germany, September 25, 2011, http://www.catholiceducation.org/en/culture/catholic-contributions/it-is-time-for-the-church-to-set-aside-her-worldliness.html.

23. Benedict XVI, "Meeting with Catholics Engaged in the Life of the Church and Society," http://w2.vatican.va/content/benedict-xvi/en/speeches/2011/september/documents/hf_ben-xvi_spe_20110925_catholics-freiburg.html.

24. de Lubac, *Méditation*, 144: my translation; see *Splendor*, 167.

25. See the remarkable homily that Pope Francis preached to his fellow Jesuits on the Feast of Saint Ignatius, July 31, 2013, http://w2.vatican.va/content/francesco/en/homilies/2013/documents/papa-francesco_20130731_omelia-sant-ignazio.html.

26. de Lubac, *Méditation*, 201: my translation; see *Splendor*, 232.

27. The original French subtitle of de Lubac's *Catholicism* is "The Social Aspects of the Dogma."

28. Joseph Ratzinger, *Pilgrim Fellowship of Faith: The Church as Communion*, trans. Henry Taylor (San Francisco: Ignatius Press, 2005), 78.

29. See http://w2.vatican.va/content/benedict-xvi/en/encyclicals/documents/hf_ben-xvi_enc_20051225_deus-caritas-est.html.

30. See http://w2.vatican.va/content/benedict-xvi/en/encyclicals/documents/hf_ben-xvi_enc_20071130_spe-salvi.html.

31. Spadaro, *A Big Heart Open to God*, 25.

32. Ibid., 26.

33. Francis, "Audience of June 12, 2013," http://w2.vatican
.va/content/francesco/en/audiences/2013/documents/papa-
francesco_20130612_udienza-generale.html.

34. Some of these concerns find expression in his article
"The Ecclesiology of the Constitution *Lumen Gentium*," in
Ratzinger, *Pilgrim Fellowship of Faith*, 125–29.

35. Quoted in Maximilian Heim, *Joseph Ratzinger: Life in the
Church and Living Theology*, trans. Michael J. Miller (San Francisco:
Ignatius Press, 2007), 523.

36. Francis, "Audience of October 22, 2014," http://w2.vati
can.va/content/francesco/en/audiences/2014/documents/papa-
francesco_20141022_udienza-generale.html.

37. For further elaboration of these points, see Robert P.
Imbelli, *Rekindling the Christic Imagination: Theological Meditations
on the New Evangelization* (Collegeville, MN: Liturgical Press,
2014).

CHAPTER 2

A CHURCH OF THE POOR

Maria Clara Bingemer

On February 11, 2013, Benedict XVI stepped down as pope, who, as Bishop of Rome, is also the head of the universal church. The chair of Peter became empty. Around the world, perplexity caught the hearts and minds of many people. The ecclesial communities of the entire world turned their eyes toward Rome where such a unique situation was taking place. Awareness of the shadows that swooped down on this institution, the oldest in the history of humankind, became clear. Painful and obscure facts that the media revealed led to desolation among Catholics in every place and seeded insecurity in many. Questions were raised along with fearful expectations.

The announcement of joy (*gaudium magnum*) was made with shaking voice by the French Cardinal Tauran. The name he pronounced, Jorge Mario Bergoglio, astonished many and was questioned by others. Silence descended over Saint Peter's Square as the thousands who gathered waited for the new pope to appear. As Francis emerged on the Vatican balcony, in a joyful and quiet voice, he greeted them simply: *Buona sera* ("Good evening"). Before blessing the people, the newly elected pope asked for a blessing from them. He explained that his fellow cardinals had a tough time trying to give Rome a bishop. They had to search for him at the end of the world. He presented himself as the Bishop of Rome, Rome being the church that presides over all the other churches in charity. These first words had the power of the announcement of a new era for the church, which could now rejoice and breathe with new hope.

In his gestures, acts, and words, Pope Francis reaffirms the preferential option for the poor and the theme of the "poor church and church of the poor" in its original meaning. This topic, central to the Latin American church after the Council, is now the leitmotif of the new pontificate.

In this chapter, we will first examine the roots and origins of this ecclesial option for the poor of the Latin American church. Then we will see the most central features of Bergoglio's action as Cardinal Archbishop of Buenos Aires. Last, we will identify some points that are central for today's understanding of Pope Francis's ecclesiology.

POST–VATICAN II: A CATHOLICISM OF THE POOR

In 1965, following the Second Vatican Council that had left behind enthusiasm and hope together with some apprehension, the air had the flavor and perfume of a new spring. The whole world was involved in the reception and hermeneutics of this new way of being church, in dialogue with the world and its joys and sorrows.[1]

For the Catholic Church in Latin America, it was the beginning of a new era. The Latin American church strongly desired to be a "source church" and not only a "projection church" that repeated the church in Europe without creativity in a very different context. That was the spirit with which the Latin American bishops convoked the conference in Medellín, Colombia, in 1968.[2]

The conference gathered all the bishops of the Latin American continent together with theologians and pastoral agents. Even today, the conference is regarded as a landmark in the history of Latin American Catholicism. It was an event inspired by the Spirit of God who renewed this hemisphere, emphasizing the centrality of justice, a constitutive part of the proclamation of the gospel and of the church's mission. Consequently, the conference at Medellín inaugurated, not only for Latin America but for the world, a new way of being church consisting of service, a commitment to justice and liberation, and recovering from the margins of history a new place and prominence for the voice of the poor. The concluding document of the conference said, "This continues to be the time of Word but has turned to be also, dramatically, the time of Action."[3] The Latin American church, inspired by the Spirit, understood that now was the time to act in favor of those whose destinies were aggressively diminished by poverty.

In 1968, three years after the Second Vatican Council, the Latin American bishops stated that they wanted no longer to be a church that "reflected" the orientations and priorities issued from afar, but a church that was a *source* of new thought emerging from the Latin American context.[4] The Medellín bishops issued three major points: (1) connect the preaching of the gospel with the practice of justice; (2) consider the mysteries of Revelation from the perspective of the poor; and (3) inaugurate a new way of being a church, by gathering laypeople from the poorest parts of the continent to interpret the Bible in a transformative way.[5]

In 1979, the Latin American Conference of Bishops (CELAM) in Puebla, Mexico, reemphasized those three points, officially instituting a system of grassroots groups called Base Ecclesial Communities, ministering to the poor preferentially. This new theology was dubbed "Liberation Theology."[6] In 2007, the Fifth Conference of CELAM, meeting in Aparecida, Brazil, brought attention to the importance of ministering to the poor. In his opening speech, Pope Benedict XVI reconfirmed this option as an evangelical one, no longer to be questioned in terms of its validity, for it is implicitly already contained in a christological faith in God, who became poor for us to enrich us with his poverty.[7]

Gustavo Gutiérrez defines *liberation theology* as a critical reflection on Christian praxis, with the poor being the center of Christian life.[8] Gutiérrez affirms nevertheless that it neither starts nor departs from a simple critical analysis of reality, but moves instead from a mystical experience: a deep encounter with the Lord in the face of the poor. From here, a method was developed: to see, judge, and act.[9] In an oppressed context, there can be no theology without social analysis (to see), which must then be tied to the prophetic challenge of Scripture (to judge). The transformative stage (to act) will then give rise to, inspire, and guide the commitment and political positions of Christians.[10] This theology was not meant to remain in books and academic courses, but instead to relate back to the poor and help put into action their process of liberation. Liberation theology sought to build a new society by struggling alongside the poor to make them the subjects of their own history.[11]

It is worth saying that this concept was not invented by liberation theology. Because the poor are at the very heart of the gospel, throughout the entire history of the church, the poor have been central as the objects of a privileged love in Christian social teaching, in the reflections of the fathers of the church[12] and in the teaching and witness of the saints and mystics. The novelty here is that the Catholic Church in Latin America inaugurated a movement within the church that had a strong social and political impact on the configuration of Latin American society. The attention to the poor was not a task for individuals. Rather, it represented a complete commitment of the church, which reaffirmed the Second Vatican Council, the move toward a greater engagement with the world, and the definition of the church as the "church of the poor."[13]

In the middle of the twentieth century, when the process of secularization deepened, everybody waited for enlightenment from Pope John XXIII, who spoke powerfully of the church of the poor. Now Pope Francis places at the core of his teaching the importance for the church to be a church for the poor and of the poor, to take special care of the poor, to move to the margins. On that track, Latin American theology has walked during the five decades that followed the Second Vatican Council.

POVERTY AND INJUSTICE

Together with economic poverty, there is also in Latin America a sociocultural poverty. This element was very much stressed by the "theology of the people" (*teología del pueblo*), a theology that was very dear to the Archbishop of Buenos Aires, Jorge Mario Bergoglio. The "theology of the people" was, according to Gustavo Gutiérrez, a stream with its own characteristics within liberation theology.[14] The most important figures in the first generation of this theology are: Virginia Raquel Azcuy,[15] Lucio Gera,[16] and Rafael Tello.[17] Figuring into subsequent generations of a theology of the people are, among others, J. C. Scannone and Carlos Galli. The proper task of this theology is to work with cultural and symbolic mediations as hermeneutical choices.

Scannone defines the steps for this theology as follows:

1. To take as the point of departure the Latin American peoples, the original ones (*pueblos originarios*), in whose wisdom religion is frequently inculturated.
2. To make preferential use of the historical-cultural analysis as a method to interpret and judge the historical and social reality of the poor in the light of faith.
3. To use such human sciences as history, cultural anthropology, or sciences of religion (but also symbols and narratives) in a more synthetic and hermeneutical way without despising the analytical sciences.
4. To critique the use of the Marxist instrument of analysis, considered insufficiently critical from a theological perspective. The poor have, nevertheless, a special place within the central categories of a *teología del pueblo*: people, popular religion, culture.

Liberation theologians, however, never ignored the importance of cultural poverty. It includes racial, ethnic, and sexual oppression and discrimination. In addition, for Afro-descendants, indigenous peoples, and women, the difficulty of living increases. This difficulty is not independent of socioeconomic reality, but in developing countries, it is at least in part a product of it. That is the reason why liberation theology chose to face socioeconomic poverty as a central priority.

What emerged was a new way of doing theology, identified mainly as liberation theology, even if there were some nuances of understanding it differently, as in the case of Argentina. The "theology of the people" is mostly an Argentinian phenomenon, while the rest of the continent mainly adhered to the more mainstream form of liberation theology.

THE IMPACT OF BERGOGLIO

In Argentina, the grassroots priests (*curas villeros*)[18] have existed since 1969 as a team created by Cardinal Aramburu. Nevertheless, when Monseñor Bergoglio took over the archdiocese, he wanted to send more priests and resources to those communities, while also creating more parishes there. He enlarged the number of priests working there full time from 8 to 22 in order to assist the 180,000 people who live in those precarious populations on the peripheries of Buenos Aires.[19]

Cardinal Bergoglio was very close to those priests, giving them support when the military governments or the police or anyone else, including drug dealers, threatened them. He walked there alone, surprising those who worked at the "villas." The fact is that the cardinal was really in love with the popular religiosity of the people, and so he sought to be present to them as often as possible. It was very common, according to the priests, that during the youth pilgrimages to Lujan—the most famous Marian shrine in Argentina—Bergoglio himself would be the one who went to hear the confessions of the young pilgrims who filled the basilica. He also had the habit of arriving suddenly, without prior warning, at a popular shelter or at one of the feasts in honor of the Virgin Mary in one of the poor neighborhoods where the priests were working.

Bergoglio's closeness and commitment to this group of priests perplexed many when he was Cardinal Archbishop of Buenos Aires since he was thought to have a political position more compatible with the center and even with the right wing, a position sharply critical of the Kirchner government. These were the priests, after all, who regarded themselves as the spiritual heirs of Father Mugica, the icon of the militancy of the seventies in the country.[20]

What influenced the *curas villeros* was clearly liberation theology, the most important school of theology in Latin America, whose main references were Gustavo Gutiérrez from Peru and Leonardo Boff from Brazil. This theology ran into significant difficulties with the Vatican; it was accused of adopting Marxism because of its use of Marxist categories of analysis for the diagnosis of reality. Today, the priests who work in the "villas" are closer to the school of theology named *"teología del pueblo."*[21]

One of the priests who worked at the villas during the military dictatorship said that they were Peronists because the people were. Father Pepe—a priest who was very much admired by the pope and who inspired Pope Francis's famous insistence that priests have to smell like their sheep—adds, "It was another time and the challenges were according to that moment: today we deal with the violence of delinquency and drug dealing, and not with politics. Those are new challenges, but the spirit is the same." This wise definition of Father Pepe seems to synthesize in a very pertinent way what is at the core of Pope Francis's proposal for a church of the poor and for the poor.

CONCLUSION

The main characteristic of Pope Francis's pontificate is the deep conviction that the poor lie at the heart of Christianity; they

35

are not an appendix to the gospel. That is why he wants to change, through his gestures, words, and preaching, the lifestyles and the consumer habits of the faithful. His struggle is tireless against the culture of waste; it was so in Buenos Aires and it is so now in Rome.

We could say without fear that his theology is a liberation theology as he puts Christian mercy as the central goal of the church. At the center of the church that Bergoglio desires are the rights of the last and the least of the earth, without which there is no human dignity. Faith that operates by charity will have to find good ways of doing politics that resist unregulated capitalism, individualistic religion, and corporate interests.[22]

For him, then, attention to the poor is not exclusive or reductive. On the contrary, it is the only promise of a universal attention. It is not only that war generates poverty, but also that hunger and poverty generate those poisoned fruits that are war and violence. A few days after being elected, he said to a crowd of journalists: "How I would like a church that is poor and for the poor." In *Evangelii gaudium*, his apostolic exhortation outlining the basic program of his pontificate, he states,

> Our commitment does not consist exclusively in activities or programs of promotion and assistance; what the Holy Spirit mobilizes is not an unruly activism, but above all an attentiveness which considers the other "in a certain sense as one with ourselves." This loving attentiveness is the beginning of a true concern for their person which inspires me effectively to seek their good. This entails appreciating the poor in their goodness, in their experience of life, in their culture, and in their ways of living the faith. True love is always contemplative, and permits us to serve the other not out of necessity or vanity, but rather because he or she is beautiful above and beyond mere appearances: "The love by which we find the other pleasing leads us to offer him

something freely." The poor person, when loved, "is esteemed as of great value," and this is what makes the authentic option for the poor differ from any other ideology, from any attempt to exploit the poor for one's own personal or political interest. Only on the basis of this real and sincere closeness can we properly accompany the poor on their path of liberation. Only this will ensure that "in every Christian community the poor feel at home. Would not this approach be the greatest and most effective presentation of the good news of the kingdom?" Without the preferential option for the poor, "the proclamation of the Gospel, which is itself the prime form of charity, risks being misunderstood or submerged by the ocean of words which daily engulfs us in today's society of mass communications." (EG 199)

This is Francis's church: poor and for the poor. To love and serve the poor should then be the purest and greatest joy of the missionary disciples that all Christians are called to be.

NOTES

1. Cf. *Gaudium et spes* 1.

2. Cf. the Concluding Document of the Conference of Latin American Bishops in Medellín, http://www.celam.org/conferencia_medellin.php. See some excerpts in English at http://www.geraldschlabach.net/medellin-1968-excerpts/.

3. Introduction to the Concluding Document of the Conference of Latin American Bishops in Medellín, 1968.

4. On this point, see the reflection of the great Brazilian philosopher Henrique de Lima Vaz, "Igreja-reflexo vs. Igreja-fonte," *Cadernos Brasileiros*, no 46, (Mar/Abr, 1968): 17–22.

5. Cf. The Concluding Document of the Conference of Latin American Bishops in Medellín, 1968. See also the comments and reflections after the Concluding Document of the Conference of Latin American Bishops in Medellín, for instance,

Agenor Brighenti, "A opção pelos pobres e a urgencia da missao," in www.revistamissoes.org.br.

6. See Clodovis Boff, "A originalidade historica de Medellín," http://www.servicioskoinonia.org/relat/203p.htm.

7. See Pope Benedict, Address in Aparecida, May 13, 2007.

8. Gustavo Gutiérrez, *A Theology of Liberation: History, Politics and Salvation* (New York: Orbis, 1971).

9. The lay movement, Catholic Action (Action Catholique), born in France and very strong in Latin America in the 1950s and the 1960s, systematized this methodology. It helped Christians who were socially engaged in the search for a critical understanding of their reality to make a commitment for transformative action.

10. The method of this theology is inductive and not deductive. Rather than beginning with Revelation and ecclesial tradition to develop theological interpretations to be applied to life, the liberationist method begins with the realities of poverty and exclusion, and the commitment to liberation, which then gives rise to a theological reflection and invitation to transformative action of this same reality. It brings also a critique of modern theology and its pretention to universality, considering it Eurocentric and unconnected to the reality of poor and peripheral countries.

11. See Leonardo and Clodovis Boff, "A Concise History of Liberation Theology," http://www.landreform.org/boff2.htm.

12. See the works of Ambrose, Chrysostom, and the like.

13. The phrase "church of the poor" was first used by Pope John XXIII in his inaugural address to the Fathers of the Vatican Council in 1962, *Gaudet mater ecclesia.*

14. Gustavo Gutiérrez, *La fuerza histórica de los pobres* (Lima: CEP, 1979), 377.

15. "Teología ante el reto de la pobreza una perspectiva latinoamericana desde las mujeres," texto en elaboración, 2002.

16. Lucio Gera is considered as the main inspiration for this school of theology in Argentina. Cf. R. Ferrara and C. Galli, eds., *Presente y futuro de la teología en Argentina. Homenaje a Lucio Gera* (Buenos Aires: Paulinas, 1997).

17. I follow here Azcuy in her article quoted above regarding the contribution of V. M. Fernández rescuing the itinerary of that

theology: "Creo que nadie se acercó teológicamente al pobre como el padre Rafael Tello. Él es—junto con Lucio Gera—una de las grandes figuras de la 'teología de la cultura popular'. Por eso me parece injusto, aun cuando a él pueda desagradarle todo homenaje, que casi nunca se lo mencione cuando se habla de la teología argentina" ("I believe nobody got so close theologically to the poor as Fr. Rafael Tello. He is—together with Lucio Gera—one of the great figures of the 'popular culture' theology. That is why it seems unjust to me even when he can be displeased with every praise, that he is almost never mentioned when we speak of Argentinian theology"); cf. *Con los pobres hasta el fondo. El pensamiento teológico de Rafael Tello*, in V. R. Azcuy (coord.), *Semillas del siglo XX*, Proyecto 36 (2000): 187–205, at 187.

18. They are referred to this way because they live and work at the "villas," situated at the margins and poor peripheries of the city, with all sorts of problems: homelessness, food scarcity, drug addictions, and so on.

19. See the article in *La Nacion*, a very important newspaper of Buenos Aires: "Curas villeros: predicadores de la teología del pueblo," http://www.lanacion.com.ar/1262615-curas-villeros-predicadores-de-la-teologia-del-pueblo.

20. In a book published last year, F. Ambrogetti and S. Rubin, *El Jesuita* (Buenos Aires: Vergara, 2014), Bergoglio himself, answering those who questioned him about the role he had during the difficult 1970s, said about Francisco Jalics and Orlando Yorio, the two Jesuits who worked in the Villa del Bajo Flores who disappeared under his period as provincial: "I did what I could with the age and the little influence I had."

21. *La Nacion*, footnote 24.

22. See about that G. Galeazzi, "Dois anos. Papa Francisco, os pobres e o aguilhão do sistema econômico," in IHU Online, March 9, 2015. The article was originally published in the Italian newspaper *La Stampa*, March 5, 2015. The translation is by Benno Dischinger.

CHAPTER 3

EVANGELIZATION, INCULTURATION, AND POPULAR RELIGION

Cecilia González-Andrieu

SPEAKING OF FRANCISCO[1]

His chosen name is Francis, Latin Americans sometimes refer to him as el Papa Bergoglio,[2] and since his election, I have called him Pope Francisco. This name in Spanglish fits a man who is uniquely deserving of the title *Pontifex*—bridge-builder and bridge person. In this chapter, we examine the overly used and sometimes tired concepts of "evangelization" and "inculturation" through the refreshing uniqueness of Pope Francisco's articulation of popular religion/*religiosidad popular* and the problems and promises it represents. As a Latin American theologian and a Jesuit, Pope Francisco understands, values, and loves this vital and neglected part of the church's life. As a Jesuit, he belongs to a line of evangelizers who undertook the work of mission by going out into the whole world, being respectful of the customs, traditions, and beliefs of the new human groups they encountered, and enlisting the aid of aesthetic objects and rituals in the proclamation of the gospel. The Jesuits understood that what was artful could delight, teach, and move (*delectare, docere,* and *movere*).[3] Francisco's appreciation for popular religion is directly connected to his identity because, as he stresses, *religiosidad popular* is itself an expression of identity.

POPULAR RELIGIOSITY

Pope Francisco's papacy has brought to the consciousness of the world (and I mean the world, not just the church)[4] an appreciation for practices referred to as "popular religiosity," but often disparaged in societies with iconoclastic and dualistic tendencies. "We must begin with an anthropology that considers the human person as a whole made of body-spirit, open to the infinite."[5] *La religiosidad popular* appears in Pope Francisco's writings and public practices as the way in which the most defenseless among us may hold the key to a revitalized life in Christ for all people of good will. In *Evangelii gaudium,* he notes that the thirst for spirituality in the contemporary world is often answered in ways that amount to a type of spiritual consumerism fostering individualism. He does not blame the culture for providing these, nor does he blame people for seeking them, rather he places the blame on the "official" church.

> If [people] don't find in the church a spirituality that will heal them, liberate them, fill them with life and peace while at the same time calling them to a communion of solidarity and the fruitfulness of mission, they will end up deceived by proposals that do not humanize and do not glorify God.
>
> The forms that are proper to *la religiosidad popular* are incarnated, because they germinated from the enfleshing of Christian faith in a people's culture. Because of this they include a personal relationship not with harmonizing energies but with God, *Jesucristo,*[6] Mary, a saint. They have flesh, they have faces. They are well

suited to nurture gifts of relationality and not individualist escapism. (EG 89–90)[7]

In many of his writings, what Francisco's critiques make clear is that the perpetuation of a false dichotomy pitting "official" rites and devotions against "popular" ones overlooks the complexity of human longing and human history. "Official rites" arose from the religious creativity of discrete groups of Christians, and therefore were simply homegrown before they were "official." These practices were born out of the desire for God and for ways to enact that desire in relationship. As church, we need to recognize this same desire for God in our contemporaries, and open ourselves to the creativity this involves, otherwise, as the old song goes, we will be "looking for love in all the wrong places."

Pope Francisco's attention to uniqueness, embodiment, and relationality—three of the principal features of popular religion—is indispensable for a man who understands himself as facing "a particular challenge in being Shepherd of a church without borders, a church that knows itself mother of all" (EG 210). The question of the church as one and as many is at the very center of the tension presented by evangelization, which is the sharing of the *one* gospel with the entire world. How does the unchanging oneness of the Christian proclamation penetrate a truly global church to spill out and beguile the whole world? How does the church enact the mandate to preach the gospel to the ends of the earth (Acts 1:8), when "the ends of the earth" is literal and not an abstraction? Does a church without borders connote a Roman church so centralized and totalizing that in the service of "unity," all difference is erased? Or, as Francisco's oft-evoked image of *the church as mother* suggests, does borderless denote the unconditional embrace the church offers to all, the differences in each of her children making them singularly and uniquely beloved? Is difference actually beautiful, and are borders and hierarchies just our absurd attempts to fight against what is most human, our multiply expressed uniqueness, our embodiment, and our need of one another?

Francisco enacts the answer to this question in his practice of confronting us with our messy many-ness as human beings and communities. "The Gospel," he insists with his accustomed boldness, "is always inviting us to run the risk of encountering the other's face, with a physical presence that confronts us with its pain and its supplications, with its infectious joy that spreads in the constant encounter of one body with another body" (EG 88). Francisco insists that the church as people of God cannot be imagined as a monolithically oppressive abstraction, but rather "incarnates in the peoples of the earth, each one of which has its own culture" (EG 115). Here we see the link between the oneness of the gospel and the "innumerable languages and traditions" of the world, which demands the practice we have come to call "inculturation" and which the church recognized as vital in the documents of the Second Vatican Council.[8] What Francisco's renewal of attention to "popular religion" adds is a very efficient "how" to the question of inculturation. *Religiosidad popular* is a multicontinent, multicentury case study, if you will, shedding light on "our difficulty to recreate the mystical embrace required of faith in a religiously plural stage" (EG 70).

The process of inculturation is required of a church awake to the astonishing variety of humans on our planet, and that respects their uniqueness. In the end, Francisco observes, "Inculturation is the process by which faith becomes culture,"[9] and we can add that popular religiosity is the very working out of this process. As Francisco notes, the meaning of the word *culture* has completely changed in the decades between the first meeting of CELAM in Rio de Janeiro (1955) and the fifth in Aparecida (2007) where he was a principal contributor.[10] Francisco stresses that in the Aparecida document, the word *culture* appears about seventy times and this coincides with the positive role accorded to popular religion in marked contrast with the first writings of the Latin American church.[11] In this development, Francisco understands the inextricable connection between the desire for a renewed evangelizing spirit in the church and the need to embrace one of

44

its most powerful and enduring expressions—popular religion. Francisco's appreciative respect for the power of culture is part of who he is, "religiosity from its variety of expressions, so alive and meaningful can come to the rescue of the human person, their identity and their vocation to live."[12]

THE CULTURE

Jorge Bergoglio, the Argentinean grandson of Italian immigrants who, following the First World War, had braved an uncertain voyage seeking a new life in the land of America,[13] was scarcely in his twenties during the Second Vatican Council and has a nuanced sense of "culture" marked by his regard for its centrality in the God-human dialogue of history. If the church understands being evangelized as inhabiting fully an identity that is uniquely defined by the gospel, and inculturation as the process that gets us there, then we must inquire into the very form of our human inhabiting in the world: culture.

Pope Francisco, who famously asked his brother priests to "be shepherds with the smell of sheep,"[14] lives with intentionality in the particularity of a culture, while also embracing with excitement its multiple incarnations. He chooses to inhabit the world in a very specific way, knowing that his dialogue with the world rises out of Jorge/Francisco and not a universal pope who lives outside of his own humanity. Through his *cotidianidad* (daily life)[15]—traveling in a used car, living in a guest house for pilgrims, speaking colorful Argentinian Spanish that is full of idiomatic word plays or turns of a phrase, sipping the traditional maté, and embracing the "least" at every opportunity he gets—he is a testimony to the communicative power of bodylines and the indispensability of context.

As a true shepherd, Pope Francisco delights in using his body. Through gestures layered with symbolism, he engenders a constant state of *asombro* (revelatory surprised wonder) in his fellow humans.[16] This *asombro*, attested to by the unprecedented media attention his every act receives, invites reflection and may result in appreciative emulation of the one he resolutely follows, *Jesucristo*. This is a conscious and deliberate choice that foregrounds how this particular pope understands the human condition as at all times *lived* (not merely thought about) in a state of wakeful discovery.[17] Francisco speaks of the gospel as being *encarnado* (taking on flesh) within a culture, and because of this, "transmitted in forms so varied that it is impossible to describe them or catalogue them where the People of God with its innumerable gestures and signs is a collective subject" (EG 129). For him, our intimate relationship with the God of life, of joy, and of history depends primarily on fruitfully encountering what is real.

Before proceeding further, two key terms require nuancing in order to understand what is meant by *religiosidad popular*. In Spanish, *popular* differs from its English cognate. *Popular* from the Latin *popularis* refers to that which belongs to the common people, the "lower" classes in a socioeconomically stratified society. We could certainly say that most of the time, Jesus was involved with this very group in his own society, and accordingly, we could even call Jesus' movement, *un movimiento popular*. The other term, *pueblo* can also be confusing as it can simply mean a small town (*el pueblo de Los Angeles*), or a people (*el Pueblo Argentino*). However, as used in relation to popular religion, *el pueblo* refers precisely to the common people, the "lower" classes. *El pueblo* are those lacking economic and educational advantages, and in some colloquialisms, it is used pejoratively as in the English *plebeian* through the dismissive terms *el populacho* or *la plebe*. It is this discarded and "disinherited" *pueblo* that generates, from the depth of their faith, "a church born from the people (*una Iglesia que nace del pueblo*), the truest expression of which is *religiosidad popular* or *religión popular*."[18]

As is now apparent, the translations "popular religion" or "popular religiosity" fail to properly communicate the phenomenon. *Religiosidad popular* is also a term that unfortunately, as well-meaning as it may be, perpetuates class-consciousness and in many cases, dissimulates disdainful attitudes toward those "lower class" ways of being religious. As Orlando Espín sagely points out, "In Catholic theological circles, popular religion is either treated as an example of what should *not* be, or it is simply ignored as of no value for the serious theological enterprise."[19]

The designation "popular religion" also neglects the distinction between the instances where what is being described is what is practiced among certain discrete groups of Catholic Christians or by persons of other Christian denominations or those of other religions. Clearly, the religious practices of the lower segments of society can be appreciated in other Christian and also non-Christian groups, as can some variations on it, such as civil religion, represented in monuments, parades, and songs. To complicate matters more, the phenomenon of popular religion is not limited to the unique blending of influences of the Spanish-speaking world, but is recognizable in many other communities. Even if we were to limit the term to the Spanish-speaking world, we would have to recognize the multitude of strands of influences these practices denote. To the parent of Iberian Catholicism, we would add its Muslim and Jewish strands, and to the parent of the communities encountered in the American continent or inserted into its family tree, the extensive variety of indigenous traditions and their African counterparts. Pope Francisco, working from his particular context, is most often referring to *religiosidad popular* as he knows it intimately in the Spanish-speaking world and consequently in its Catholic expressions. He gets very close to providing a definition of it when he says,

> *La religiosidad popular* is simply the way of being religious of believers who must express publicly, with sincere and simple spontaneity, their Christian faith, received from generation to generation, and which has formed the life and customs of the whole people.[20]

We simply lack a term that honors all of these nuances or acknowledges that this is ultimately an aesthetic undertaking enmeshed in the work of the senses. Taking into account the complications recounted above, a definition that may bridge the differences without ignoring these for what we call "popular religiosity" is simply *human creativity in search of an encounter with the divine*. Thus, at its root, *religiosidad popular* is artfulness. We can then coherently assign to it the authority and respect Pope John Paul II gives to the creative impulse:

> Every genuine artistic intuition goes beyond what the senses perceive and, reaching beneath reality's surface, strives to interpret its hidden mystery. The intuition itself springs from the depths of the human soul, where the desire to give meaning to one's own life is joined by the fleeting vision of beauty and of the mysterious unity of things.[21]

Human creativity is always culturally expressed, received, and transmitted, and thus we return to the intricate meaning of culture.

CULTURE, GOSPEL, AND LIFE

First, Francisco understands culture as creating settings that are particular to certain groups. These sociocultural realities must be sought beyond our own "territory" and most urgently in the "peripheries" (EG 30). Culture is specifically *ours* and also specifically *other*, and as such is the vehicle for revelatory encounter par excellence. To appreciate *popular religiosity* is to get to know the other in the way they express their yearning for God, to meet their otherness in their religious creativity, and thus to open ourselves up to transformation and renewal. It is likewise to offer ourselves, in the vulnerability of our own expressions, to be known as seekers of God's love.

Second, the place where the world's changing nature becomes most evident is in the rapid pace of cultural transformation, sometimes gradual, other times sudden, but always present. "Cultural changes," Francisco notes, "require we pay attention constantly so we may attempt to express the truths that do not change in a language that makes evident their permanent state of newness."[22] This view of culture achieves several aims. It legitimates the idea of process as a coherent view of human reality. This, in turn, opens the possibility that as a church, we may grow in our "understanding of the Gospel, discerning the paths of the Spirit" in a way that does not take refuge in closed and defensive postures.[23] If we are attentive to the dynamism of culture, we will not forget that faith must always be articulated as a new discovery. *Religiosidad popular* discloses that inculturation is an ongoing process requiring openness and creativity, precisely because it acts on the promise of deepening our relationship with God. A *religiosidad humana* takes the search for the transcendent and weaves it creatively into the cultural norms of our tradition of living faith and sacramentality.

A third oft-neglected point is that "culture" and its multiplicity does not only exist outside the church, but indeed within it. Cultural dialogue includes the interior as well as the exterior, and the inculturation of the gospel may need urgent attention among those assumed to be evangelized. Encountering the freshness of new and unexpected forms can propel evangelization in the church's internal life.[24]

Closely connected is a fourth consideration, which Francisco elaborates through his intimate understanding of the theological insights introduced by CELAM. It was through articulating "the option for the poorest that particular churches were able to get closer to the multifaceted religio-cultural reality of the continent."[25] This is of fundamental importance in understanding how Francisco links evangelization, inculturation, and popular religion. He stresses that it was only by providing "space for the poor to be and speak" that the Latin American part of the church was able to "rediscover a hidden church, made up from the remnants of over 2,600 native peoples…along with more than two million descendants of African peoples."[26] Without the attentiveness to the poor enunciated by CELAM and centrally articulated today by

Francisco, the Catholic Church's astoundingly diverse global identity remains hidden. The option for the poor requires that the creative ways of being religiously Catholic of the *pueblo* be respected and encouraged. Globally, the majority of the people of God of the church come from the *pueblo*; they are the many, who until now have been discarded by the few.[27] Additionally, it is through incorporating the poor's ways of being religious into the church's liturgical life that the force of the gospel is rediscovered and renewed. If we dare to pay attention, the poor's faith, expressed creatively and uniquely in each corner of the globe, will evangelize the whole church.

> Popular religiosity is the faith of the common people, that becomes life and culture, is the particular mode that the *pueblo* has of living and expressing its relation to God, to the Virgin, and to the saints, in their private and intimate environments and most especially in the community.[28]

As he reflects on the concluding document of Aparecida, Bergoglio synthesizes some of the most salient features of culture: (1) Subjects create culture. This implies creativity and expression; (2) Subjects implement culture. This stresses freedom, agency, and also responsibility; (3) Subjects respond to culture. Here we note dynamism and the potency of aesthetically mediated communication; and (4) Subjects interpret their surroundings through culture.[29] This is a potent feature recognized in a theological aesthetics posture that treats cultural creativity as a *locus* of theological reflection.[30] As John Paul II expresses it,

> Every genuine art form in its own way is a path to the inmost reality of [humanity] and of the world. It is therefore a wholly valid approach to the realm of faith, which gives human experience its ultimate meaning. That is why the Gospel fullness of truth was bound from the beginning to stir the interest of artists, who by

their very nature are alert to every "epiphany" of the inner beauty of things.[31]

Religiosidad popular is a legitimate way of carrying out theological reflection, expressed in new forms but in continuity with the church's tradition of enacting a faith that wants to express its every act of seeking God's face.

THE BEAUTY OF THE GOSPEL

As he seeks God's face, Pope Francisco is primarily a lover of life, and his commitment to his ministry as the current shepherd of the Catholic Church—and as many claim, of all people of good will—stems from his most fundamental commitment to the reign of God. "To evangelize," he says with the clear conviction of much Latin American theology, "is to make the Reign of God present in the world" (EG 176). This goal of making the reign present, not as a future-only event, but as at this very moment making a "claim" on us (EG 180), is a key to both the orientation of his actions and how he understands the density of every moment of history.

For Pope Francisco, the gospel—the announcement of the in-breaking reign—is first of all beautiful (EG 42), and as such, it calls to us. The kind of complicated beauty evident in the gospel can only be made present to the world by a church able to unify in its proclamation "what is transcendent with what is immanent; what is eternal with what is *lo cotidiano*."[32] This ability to unify what appears as impossibly dichotomous is the gift of those whose expressions of faith "are born in the shadow of much suffering."[33] The gospel must help us walk that most complicated road that Pope Francisco sees beautifully expressed by the novelist Ernesto Sábato, who exclaims, "The greatest nobility of [hu]mankind is to construct its work in the midst of devastation, sustaining it tirelessly, halfway between desolation and beauty."[34] Francisco's life is lived in the presence of this kind of beauty, which, he affirms, fills us with trust through the experience of "the tenderness, beauty and joy of the love of God made present in the mestizo face of the Mother of God, the Virgin of Guadalupe."[35]

Francisco's expansive view stresses that the aesthetic forms the gospel takes through human hands must be always renewed so they may speak eloquently to particular human communities, while retaining what is immutable and never minimizing the confrontation of the cross and its darkness. Francis is emphatic that "beyond the clarity with which we perceive reasons and arguments, there are things which may be understood and valued only through the embrace that is the sister of love." He adds that any effort to pass on the faith must arise from "an evangelizing attitude, which invites the heart's embrace by its nearness, its love and its testimony" (EG 42). Such an effective inculturation calls for a respectful engagement with the complex phenomena of popular religion, especially because it is "our saints who inculturated the Gospel in the lives of our peoples" (EG 233). It is the people's continued memory of these saints as reenacted in their devotional lives that keeps such an evangelizing process alive.

Francisco situates himself at the very center of a self-consciously expansive church community, which he has characterized as a mother that excludes no one. From there, we see his intentional inhabiting of his humanity in his insistence on performing "deeds," thus underscoring the unity of faith and practice. As he eloquently states, "What is real is superior to ideas" (EG 233). He answers the critics of popular religion who allege that it lacks (social) commitment, saying,

> The mode that is proper to *religiosidad popular* is marked by the heart, faith is determined through sentiment… [and] the sentiments of the heart impel the faith to express itself in gestures and acts of tenderness, with God and with our siblings. What is felt in the human heart does not contradict the deepest experiences of the spirit.[36]

This is a clear indicator of Francisco's dual Latin American and Jesuit identity. *Religiosidad popular* has been doing the work of inculturation for centuries, extending the evangelizing work of the Christians whose stories and devotions first embodied the gospel in a particular time and place. The communities that pass along these creative human ways of seeking the divine continue to enact in history; the God-human story. They are often the "least" among us, and at this time of history, where the world is searching for meaning and for purpose, their creative ways of being religious may hold the answer to falling in love with the God they so clearly know and seek. "Faith is not an idea, a philosophy or an ideology. Faith comes from a personal encounter with *Jesucristo*, the son of God made flesh. The person who discovers the love of God in their life will never be the same."[37]

NOTES

1. All translations from the Spanish are the author's. Gender-specific language such as "man" for "humanity," has been translated as gender-neutral language, which is more faithful to its meaning. The use of Spanish throughout this chapter serves to make several important points: First, Pope Francisco's Latin American identity is central to his theological thought and his pastoral practice. Second, in this new century, Latin America/the Caribbean is the region with the largest number of Catholics in the world. Third, even in the United States, Spanish-speaking Catholics and their descendants are at once the oldest group of Catholics established in the region and the largest single Catholic community today. The U.S. Latino Catholic community is thus the quintessential bridge community for the entire American hemisphere and represents a formidable resource for the American church.

2. See especially the essays from *Radio Vaticana en Español* for the naming of Papa Bergoglio.

3. Gauvin A. Bailey, *Art on the Jesuit Missions in Asia and Latin America, 1542–1773* (Toronto: University of Toronto Press, 1999), 6, 8.

4. In his writings, Francisco often uses the idiom *"todo el mundo"* literally, "the whole world," which in regular usage, also means "everyone."

5. Here Francisco appears to refer to mind/body dualism, one of the difficult legacies of Christianity's accommodation to the Hellenistic world. See "Inculturación y religiosidad popular" (IRP) from Cardinal Jorge Bergoglio, "Cultura y Religiosidad Popular" (CRP), January 19, 2008.

6. There is no equivalent translation in English for the Spanish way of referring to Jesus Christ, *Jesucristo*. This is a theologically important linguistic choice that constantly underscores the unity of divine-human and resists separation in Christ and in human persons between what is spirit and what is body.

7. Note the translation directly from the Spanish text, which "sounds" much more like how Pope Francisco speaks. The official English-language translations of texts from Pope Francisco often suffer from defaulting into standard English phrasing, losing much of the vibrancy inherent in his very particular voice. Clearly, if we are speaking of inculturation, the difficulties posed by the uniqueness of a language, the specificity of a people's ancestral imagery, and the evocative nature of all speech point to the efficacy of adopting a stance discouraging monolinguality. Wherever ecclesial communities, cities, and countries are invited to cultivate this most efficient way of getting to know "the other" by learning a second language, the reality of a "church without borders" will be more evident and potent.

8. Although the Documents of the Second Vatican Council never use the term *inculturation*, the contours of the concept as it developed later are certainly present.

9. "Inculturación de la fe," IRP.

10. CELAM is the Conference of Latin American Bishops, Consejo Episcopal Latinoamericano, landmark documents reviewed by Francisco are produced at Medellín (1968), Puebla (1979), Santo Domingo (1992), and Aparecida (2007).

11. "El camino recorrido," IRP.

12. "Inculturación de la fe," IRP.

13. "The origin of the word 'nostalgia'—from the Greek *nostos*, homecoming, and *algos*, pain—has to do with a yearning to return...." Francisco quoted in, Francesca Ambrogetti and Sergio Rubin, *Pope Francis: Conversations with Jorge Bergoglio* (New York: G. P. Putnam's Sons, 2010), 6–7. In my writing, I use "America" to

designate the continent and the many nations it represents all of which are "American" and refer to the United States specifically as that particular land designated by the present geopolitical borders with Canada to the North and Mexico to the South, but which has no legitimate right to call itself "America" and its inhabitants "Americans" to the exclusion of the rest of the continent.

14. "Santa Misa Crismal Homilía del Santo Padre Francisco," Holy Thursday, March 28, 2013, http://w2.vatican.va/content/francesco/es/homilies/2013/documents/papa-francesco_20130328_messa-crismale.html.

15. *Lo cotidiano*, the meaning-charged stuff of daily existence, is a central theological category in Latino theologies; consequently, I choose not to translate the term, as the concept is much richer than what can be conveyed by "daily life."

16. For my development of the category of *asombro* in theological aesthetics, see *Bridge to Wonder: Art as a Gospel of Beauty* (Waco, TX: Baylor, 2012), 36–7.

17. Pope Francisco has little patience for "theorizing" or for speaking in abstractions, especially about and to those who are suffering. Ambrogetti and Rubin, *Pope Francis: Conversations with Jorge Bergoglio*, 28.

18. "El camino recorrido," IRP. Here Francisco is referring particularly to the insights of the documents from the Conference of Latin American Bishops at Medellín.

19. Orlando O. Espín, *The Faith of the People: Theological Reflections on Popular Catholicism* (Maryknoll, NY: Orbis Books, 1997), 64. Espín is one of the leading scholars studying popular religion. The reader is referred to his excellent and extensive body of work.

20. "Inculturación y religiosidad popular," IRP.

21. "Letter of His Holiness John Paul II to Artists," April 4, 1999.

22. Ibid., 41.

23. Ibid., 45.

24. "El Camino Recorrido," IRP.

25. Ibid.

26. Ibid.

27. In the United States, this recognition is particularly crucial as the Catholic Church becomes majority Latino/a. Whether among the ranks of the disenfranchised poor, working class, or middle class, a goal of Latino/a Christian theology is to continually remind the community of its "non-innocent" history in order to foster action-oriented solidarity with every other disenfranchised community around the globe.

28. "Inculturacion y Religiosidad Popular," IRP.

29. IRP.

30. For a succinct introduction to theological aesthetics, please see Cecilia González-Andrieu, "Theological Aesthetics and the Art of John August Swanson," *Arts, the Journal of the Society for the Arts in Religious and Theological Studies* 21, no. 2 (United Theological Seminary, 2010): 14–17.

31. John Paul II, "Letter to Artists," 6. The entire document is an elaboration of how human creativity can be an act of theologizing.

32. "Inculturación y religiosidad popular," IRP.

33. Ibid.

34. Ibid.

35. Ibid.

36. Ibid.

37. Ibid.

CHAPTER 4

RE-ENGAGING THE PEOPLE OF GOD

Gerard Mannion

THE BACKGROUND

Whereas the previous five popes each played a role at the Second Vatican Council (1962–65) in one form or another, Jorge Bergoglio was far away from Rome, undergoing Jesuit formation and teaching at a school.[1] But the Council soon came to have an enormous impact throughout Latin America in general and gave great impetus to the emergent theology of liberation that was equally energized and encouraged by the new collective ecclesial vision of the Latin American bishops through their regional organization CELAM (Consejo Episcopal Latinoamericano).

Matters in the Argentinian church were somewhat more complex than in many other postconciliar contexts—some reforms took a while to filter down throughout parts of the Argentinian church. In some respects, this situation was reflected in the experiences of the young Jesuit, soon to be catapulted into the thankless role of provincial of a divided Jesuit province.[2]

Despite its idiosyncrasies, the church in postconciliar Argentina was not alone in experiencing divisions, and the Council itself was a source of many such divisions in different

57

parts of the world. Indeed, even throughout the conciliar debates during Vatican II, there were tensions, factions, and disagreements among groups of church leaders and their theological advisors with regard to what should be the outcomes of this Council and what its message should be to the faithful throughout the Catholic Church and to the wider world community. Some pressed for stronger reaffirmations of longstanding perspectives and interpretations of church teachings. Others wished for a church more engaged with the wider world, opening its doors and embracing renewal and reform in line with the vision indicated by Pope John XXIII in calling the Council. They also hoped for the church's teaching to take into account the needs and developments of more recent times and for that teaching to be expressed in terms more intelligible to those times. There were lively discussions over so many issues.[3]

Before the final session of the Second Vatican Council had even closed, a battle was already underway to determine how the Council's key documents should be interpreted and its vision for the church implemented. These conflicts would come to be expressed most decisively in disagreements over the self-understanding of the church.

Debates would eventually emerge about whether Vatican II itself was something of an ecclesial revolution or, on the other hand, a Council of continuity with the church's age-old traditions.[4]

When Pope Francis was elected in March 2013, many declared loudly that this pope would not depart from the outlook or agendas of his two immediate predecessors in any significant way. Early on, many continued to push the continuity agenda and, it seems, to try to canonize the ethos of Pope Benedict as if a new pope could not do otherwise than slavishly imitate his predecessor. One of the more prominent and public instances of this came in November 2013, when George Weigel told a packed plenary audience at the annual meeting of the American Academy of Religion, just three days before the release of Pope Francis's first major teaching document, *Evangelii gaudium*, that there would be nothing radical in the document whatsoever. It would be in total continuity with the ecclesial agendas of Benedict and John Paul II.

In fact, both that document and so much of Pope Francis's subsequent actions and statements have demonstrated a clear and dramatic break with the agenda and perspectives of his two immediate predecessors on many fronts. The document was a substantive statement of intent and mission. Furthermore, one of the key inspirations behind Francis's transformative vision has been the enduring ecclesiological spirit of the Second Vatican Council.

Very early on in his pontificate, Pope Francis spoke of Vatican II as a "beautiful work of the Holy Spirit."[5] He also said that throughout the church we must ask whether we have done enough to actualize what the Holy Spirit was willing the church to do through the vision of the Council. Answering his own rhetorical question in the negative, he cut to the heart of the clashes over the Council in recent decades, stating that "we celebrate this anniversary, we put up a monument but we don't want it to upset us. We don't want to change and what's more there are those who wish to turn the clock back."[6] His point was that those who resist the vision of the Council are resisting the presence and work of the Holy Spirit in the church.

In what follows, I consider a few key areas in which it appears that Pope Francis is encouraging a renewed yet updated commitment to so much of the transformative agenda of the Second Vatican Council.

PAPAL PARALLELS: THE REFORMING VISION OF VATICAN II

It is clear that Francis has sought to follow Pope John XXIII's example in many respects. He has made it clear that among the priorities for the church today is to look forward, not backward, that doctrinal minutiae and disputes are less important than living the faith and putting it into practice. He appears to want a church open to and engaged with the wider world. He accentuates what people share in common rather than what divides them. He preaches mercy, compassion, and forgiveness rather than stern admonishments and condemnations. He has stated that mercy, not moralizing, lies at the heart of the gospel.[7] And, also like John XXIII, he has said that in the church, above all else, charity must prevail in all things.[8] For Francis as for John, renewal and reform that brings the church up to date, *aggiornamento*, rather than continuity for its own sake, lie at the heart of their ecclesial agendas.

In *Evangelii gaudium*, Francis makes clear that the document offers an agenda for the church of today and the future—to identify "new paths for the Church's journey in years to come" (EG 1). For Francis, change is necessary, and he denounces as "complacent" the ecclesial standpoint that "we have always done it this way" (EG 33). Again, we hear in such statements echoes of John XXIII and his own vision for the church and especially for the Council.

The emphasis on joy is a further parallel with John—Francis wishes to encourage a more life-giving and energizing understanding, communication, and practice of the faith. He laments that "there are Christians whose lives seem like Lent without Easter" (EG 6). This, in itself, echoes John XXIII's admonishment of the "prophets of gloom" in the church and his own emphasis upon joy when opening the Council with his famous address "Mother Church Rejoices."[9]

AGGIORNAMENTO FOR COLLEGIALITY AND THE CURIA

In *Evangelii gaudium*, Francis states boldly that "the papacy and the central structures of the universal Church also need to hear the call to pastoral conversion" (no. 32). Earlier in the document, he notes that he is "conscious of the need to promote a sound 'decentralization'" in the church (no. 16) and warns against "a nostalgia for structures and customs which are no longer life-giving in today's world" (no. 108). Everything must be understood, not in the framework of rigid doctrine and canon law, but rather in terms of a "missionary key."

Again, following in the footsteps of John XXIII, Francis enters his papal ministry with the knowledge that among his top priorities must be reform of the church's own organizational structures. In particular, that reform of the Roman Curia is necessary if there is to be reform in the wider church at all. He has set about this task in an even more transparent, public, and determined fashion than John's more behind-the-scenes, diplomatic, and cautious approach to reform.

In *Evangelii gaudium*, while Francis seems to imply that this is not the place to settle contentious issues of doctrine,[10] he goes on to take a stand on a number of long-divisive ecclesiological issues. In fact, in relation to several such issues, *Evangelii gaudium* appears to take a clear and unambiguous stance.[11] For example, he has certainly appeared to take a stance on the Council's attempts to affirm a greater sense of episcopal collegiality throughout the church.

The Council's final documents were ambiguous on the ultimate nature and significance of collegiality, but there had been a strong desire on the part of the reformist majority to affirm collegiality, and many significant developments in such a direction were made. But in subsequent decades, Rome's overarching control over bishops and episcopal conferences would be reaffirmed, indeed even intensified. Francis is clearly attempting to reverse this shackling of episcopal collegiality in word and deed alike.

Throughout *Evangelii gaudium* and *Laudato si'*, he frequently cites documents issued by many different regional and national episcopal conferences around the world. Clearly this suggests he believes they have a teaching mandate, something his predecessor, while Prefect of the Congregation for the Doctrine of the Faith, denied.[12] Additionally, Francis undertook steps to ensure that the synod of bishops that met in October 2014 would be no mere talking shop for rubber-stamping preconceived conclusions.

He encouraged widespread consultation throughout the church and robust debate at the synod itself; on both counts, he would not be disappointed.

The Vatican II inspiration behind one further affirmation of a more collegial and participatory vision for ecclesial governance has gone more unnoticed. Shortly after his election, Francis swiftly established a committee of global cardinals, the so-called C8, which became C9 when Francis added his secretary of state to the group. These cardinals were selected from the world's different continents to advise him on deciding priorities for the church's future and reform, including that of the Curia—yet another, less well-known return to the spirit and will of the Council. The C9's agenda, while rightly being attentive to the "signs of the times" in our own day, has also picked up the task of addressing several key matters of unfinished business from Vatican II.

Indeed, the concept of the C9 itself might well be Pope Francis taking up the torch of reform and collegiality alike from Council father, Maximos IV Sayegh (Patriarch of the Melkite Greek Catholic Church and a cardinal from 1965). During the Council's second period (from November 6, 1963), Maximos suggested that a small group of bishops from around the world (with rotating membership) be established to help the pope in guiding the church. The Roman Curia was to be subordinate to this group, which would be a collegial solution to several dilemmas of church governance. This proposal was, in John O'Malley's words, "the first effort at the council to create a practical implementation of collegiality."[13]

CHURCH AS THE "PEOPLE OF GOD": VATICAN II'S KEY ECCLESIOLOGICAL LEGACY

The ecclesiological notion of the church as the "people of God" can be said to constitute Vatican II's core ecclesiological concept.[14] It is a guiding theme throughout many conciliar documents and, in particular, was the core focus of much of *Lumen gentium*, the

Dogmatic Constitution on the Church, where the second chapter was dedicated to the image itself and placed ahead of the chapter on the hierarchy.[15] The latter achievement, not without resistance, controversy, and compromise, was arguably one of the most significant ecclesiological breakthroughs of the Council.[16]

And yet, this ecclesial image became highly influential despite the remaining ambivalences in the conciliar documents themselves as it was widely discussed and promoted at the popular level. The concept resonated greatly, in particular, with many in the church of Latin America.[17]

The notion of the "people of God" was important because it helped introduce a way of looking at the church for new times that was not only grounded in biblical[18] and ancient ecclesial traditions, but also spoke to the contemporary world in a way that was much less patronizing or alienating than much of the official discourse of recent centuries. It especially marked a clear departure from the juridical and institutional ecclesiological discourse of the late eighteenth and especially nineteenth and early mid-twentieth centuries.

The people of God was an image of the church[19] that was less exclusivist and less affirmative of boundaries. It also helped overcome the overt emphasis in older official teachings and ecclesiological treatises upon the sense of the church as a divinely ordained hierarchy (analogous to early and mid-late modern political ideas), as a "perfect society" with the emphasis on its institutional structures.[20]

The term *people* in biblical language, *laos* (etymologically linked to the origins of the term *laity*), alongside the ecclesiological thinking that the Council inspired, helped encourage a wider sense of active engagement and participation in church roles and offices by the laity. This image challenged the idea of an active "teaching church" of the pope, bishops, and wider clergy on the one hand and the passive "learning church" of the laity on the other hand. Instead, the image of the people of God encouraged a greater sense of collaborative ministry across the church, an affirmation of the priesthood of all believers, with the laity sharing in the threefold offices of Christ as priest, prophet, and king. The sense of co-responsibility in the church was firmly underscored by the evocative implications of the church as people of God.

The concept also challenged any rigid sense of the church as the mystical Body of Christ, which had become popular again in the 1940s in ways that identified that mystical body with the institutional (Roman) Catholic Church itself. The notion of the people of God also had profound implications for ecumenical and interfaith relations.

The image of the pilgrim people of God represented a more fluid and engaging sense of the church as a community that traversed specific communities, and this had profound implications in terms of the church's affirmation of the universal salvation of all. It also was a notion with greater historical implications (locating the church as an ongoing entity across both time and space), existential implications, and sociological implications in a world so recently ravaged by national and ethnic self-interest during World War II. The church was a fluid community in the midst of other wider communities and in the midst of the ongoing story of the collective human race. The image of the church as people of God helped accentuate what Comblin has rightly termed, the "human reality of the church."[21]

The Council did not offer a rigid definition or interpretation of precisely what the term "people of God" should entail in ecclesiological terms in its entirety. This was a good thing and a familiar conciliar tactic, but such lack of determination also helped contribute to many postconciliar disagreements.

That lack of clear definition provided those who wished to challenge the concept ample room to push a different ecclesial agenda and a different preferred ecclesiology. By the mid-1980s, there were obvious attempts on the part of some in the Roman Catholic Church to shift the main ecclesiological focus from the "people of God" to the increasingly influential ecclesiology of communion (or *communio*) that was privileged in certain authoritative circles within the church, most especially in the theology of Joseph Ratzinger.[22] The church as people of God would be largely supplanted in official discourse by a very distinctive understanding of the church as *communion*. This alternative ecclesiology emphasized the necessity of local churches being secondary in foundational importance to the universal church—authentic communion with Rome became a defining feature of a church's true character. *Communio* was now promoted as the most authentic understanding of the "true" ecclesiology of the Second Vatican Council. Yet, while notions of an ecclesiology of communion (which are many and varied) were indeed debated at the Council, the sense of the church as people of God became central to the Council in a way that enveloped and subsequently shaped so many of the Council's other ecclesiological priorities and statements. The term *communion* itself appears less frequently in the conciliar documents.[23]

In particular, the 1985 Extraordinary Synod of Bishops witnessed a concerted attempt to reinterpret the Second Vatican Council's central motif as being communion as opposed to the notion of the people of God because, in the words of Matthias Scharer and Jochen Hilberath, many bishops "suspected that the notion of 'people of God' implied an inadmissible democratization of the church" and so they wished instead to emphasize the sacramentality of the church (as *mysterium*), while others "saw in this position an immunization strategy to block necessary reforms of the church's communication and decision-making structures."[24]

Slowly but surely the image of the church as people of God was challenged and then supplanted by the official *communio* ecclesiology. Many of the gains of Vatican II that were grounded upon the ecclesiology of the people of God were therefore also challenged—for example, the sense of co-responsibility in the church and a more egalitarian understanding of collaborative ministry. Episcopal collegiality was further eroded and ecumenical and interfaith dialogue undermined too, leading Comblin to comment,

> It was predictable that once the theology of the people of God had been abandoned, motivation for fomenting ecumenism would decline. People of God and ecumenism are bound together; they rise or fall together. When the theology of the people of God is abandoned, the Catholic Church folds in on itself, feels obliged to affirm its identity more emphatically, and closes the doors to the contemporary world....One of Vatican II's greatest concerns cannot be officially rejected, but in practice it is nullified.[25]

By 2000, the prevailing "official" ecclesiology in Rome had hardened further still and was far removed from the sense that the Council fathers had sought to convey with the image of the people of God. The CDF document *Dominus Iesus*[26] set back ecumenical and interfaith dialogue by some distance. Comblin predicted that a fundamental shift in official ecclesiology was the only solution that could overcome such setbacks, as people from other churches and Catholics committed to dialogue alike concluded that "no ecumenism can take place until there is a change in Rome. Only a change in ecclesiology will allow for a return to ecumenism—in tandem with the theology of the people of God."[27] Comblin's book appears prophetic in many places but perhaps nowhere more so than here. For Pope Francis has clearly and self-consciously set about revivifying the sense of the church as the people of God.

Pope Francis has deliberately rehabilitated the sense of church as "people of God" from its wilderness years of recent decades. The concept appears throughout *Evangelii gaudium* and in so many of his homilies and addresses. The Second Vatican Council's ecclesiology leaps out at the reader when Francis states that "the Church, as the agent of evangelization, is more than an organic and hierarchical institution; she is first and foremost a people advancing on its pilgrim way towards God" (EG 111). The phrase, "people of God," appears some thirteen times in the document (one more than the term "New Evangelization" appears), but in effect, it permeates every page of the document.

Francis quite deliberately chooses to reflect upon "this understanding of the church"—and, it appears, this is precisely because it offers a less fixed understanding of the church and one without rigid boundaries.[28] He demonstrates that the concept lies at the very core of his ecclesiology; "being Church *means* being God's people, in accordance with the great plan of his fatherly love. This means that we are to be *God's leaven in the midst of humanity*" (EG 111).[29] The church, then, must be a people for others, driven by mercy.[30]

In *Evangelii gaudium*, the superior tone of *Dominus Iesus* is replaced by a reaffirmation throughout of universalism. Other faiths and churches alike can bring much to Catholicism and teach it much.

And within the people of God itself there is diversity, so, like the Council, Pope Francis affirms both universalism and unity in diversity (nos. 111–13), the latter being a theme that has become the hallmark of his many statements and gestures toward encouraging ecumenical and interfaith dialogue (indeed the notion of "reconciled diversity" is one to which Francis returns time and again in his approach to such issues).[31]

Different cultures will quite naturally come to understand and express their peoples' relationship with God in different ways—grace supposes not opposes culture, therefore rigid uniformity instead of diversity is not to be the way of the church (nos. 115–19, echoing and referencing *Gaudium et spes* 36).

Francis makes clear that it is the job of the "entire" people of God to proclaim the gospel. *All are agents of evangelization.* Invoking *Lumen gentium* again, especially no. 12, Francis affirms the Council's acknowledgment of the Spirit-endowed holiness of the whole people of God whose faith will not fail even when adequate words may do so (no. 119). He states that by "virtue of their baptism, all the members of the People of God have become missionary disciples." The people of God are not to be considered "passive recipients" of some special insights from a "professional class" (no. 120).[32]

Furthermore, he states that although the church "is certainly a mystery rooted in the Trinity," reflecting the twin aspects held together also in *Lumen gentium* itself, it also "exists concretely in history as a people of pilgrims and evangelizers, transcending any institutional expression, however necessary." Its "ultimate foundation is in the free and gracious initiative of God" (EG 111). This theme also revisits conciliar debates.

Pope Francis's interpretation and the *application* of the sense of people of God are unpacked in several further areas of the document—from the underpinning of a more pluralistic understanding of the church to the transformation of church structures and that unshackling of collegiality; from the widening of the participatory nature of church offices and roles to a renewed affirmation of Christian ecumenism and interfaith dialogue, and from a renewed commitment to dialogue with and service of the wider world in general to a groundbreaking renewed commitment of the church to a preferential option for the poor. We see that the vision of *Gaudium et spes* equally permeates his vision for the church—as he has firmly committed the church to engage with the joys and hopes, as well as the griefs and anguishes of the word of these present times.

The consequences of this vision are further explicated in his speaking of a church that goes forth with doors that are "always wide open" (see, for example, nos. 15, 23, 47). Exclusion and exclusivism are to be banished from official church thought and practice.[33]

The dialogical significance of so many of Pope Francis's actions, including his many significant and open gestures, suggests that the Second Vatican Council's prioritization of dialogue has equally been made his own.

TRANSCENDING DIVISIONS AND TRANSFORMING MAGISTERIUM

The emphasis in Francis's papacy thus far upon greater consultation and dialogue, alongside increasing hints toward a radically more participatory style of teaching authority and of ecclesial governance, suggests there may also be a revolution in the understanding and exercise of magisterium in this papacy. The Second Vatican Council witnessed a number of attempts to transform the understanding and practice of magisterium in the church, but ultimately, many of these were thwarted, left unfinished at best, or subsequently undermined by later developments.

Again, like John XXIII and unlike both of their immediate predecessors, Francis does not become bogged down in doctrinal divisions. He is rather concerned with placing them in their proper perspective in the wider scheme of pastoral and missionary priorities for the church. He has denounced ecclesial vendettas and witch hunts.

Here, Francis and *Evangelii gaudium* once again echo Pope John's opening address at Vatican II that spoke of doctrinal differences dissolving as swift as the mountain mist.[34] And so, in nos. 100–101, which addresses the ecumenical situation of our times as much as it does intra-Roman Catholic divisions, we also hear echoes of the Council's Decree on Ecumenism, *Unitatis redintegratio*,[35] which stated the following:

> All in the Church must preserve unity in essentials. But let all, according to the gifts they have received enjoy a proper freedom, in their various forms of spiritual life and discipline, in their different liturgical rites, and even in their theological elaborations of revealed truth. In all things let charity prevail. If they are true to this course of action, they will be giving ever better expression to the authentic catholicity and apostolicity of the Church. (no. 4)

In fact, this passage captures the spirit of *Evangelii gaudium* in its entirety. Francis twice explicitly invokes the Council's notion of the "Hierarchy of Truths."[36] Francis also cites the actual words from Pope John's opening address to the Council, which were subsequently incorporated into *Gaudium et spes*: "At the same time, today's vast and rapid cultural changes demand that we constantly seek ways of expressing unchanging truths in a language which brings out their abiding newness. 'The deposit of the faith is one thing…the way it is expressed is another'" (no. 41). And yet Francis goes further still, suggesting that official church language and formulae may get in the way of communicating the faith itself.[37]

Throughout *Evangelii gaudium*, in keeping with its central motif of joy, we see freedom, diversity, creativity, cooperation, collaboration, and harmony affirmed, whereas rigidity, uniformity, and negativity are unmasked as being alien to the true mission of proclaiming the gospel—even a hindrance to that task.

Francis prefers the image of the harmony of multiple voices—the plurality and diversity all in service of the core message and practices at the heart of the faith. He takes care to stress the importance of freedom in all this, and acknowledges,

> For those who long for a monolithic body of doctrine guarded by all and leaving no room for nuance, this might appear as undesirable and leading to confusion. But in fact such variety serves to bring out and develop different facets of the inexhaustible riches of the Gospel. (EG 40)

The vision of church is one that is no longer by default hierarchical—in fact, one could say the ecclesiology of this pope is very much one that prioritizes the perspective from below, from the peripheries. He affirms that the "people of God" constantly evangelizes itself and that church leaders must listen to the people (EG 139).[38]

CONCLUSION

Francis consciously employs the term "people of God" in many of his homilies, addresses, interviews, and writings. Yet even when he does not explicitly mention this concept, the implications of what he is saying and doing clearly point further to this being the operative ecclesiological framework through which he understands the church and that which he wishes to promote throughout its diverse communities. It proves true, therefore, that he has swiftly reengaged the people of God in multiple ways. He has revivified the power of this evocative ecclesiological image, hence reengaging this ecclesiology. He has sought to reach out to the *actual* people of God around the globe far and wide in hitherto unprecedented ways. Furthermore, he has helped countless people, who had long since switched off from all matters ecclesial, engage once more with the church and its mission. He has restored a commitment to the life-giving sense of the church as a pilgrim people of God in both theory and practice. The ecclesiological revolution that Comblin said was necessary in 2004 may have already begun,[39] and it does indeed appear to be manifesting itself as another ecclesial instance of going "back to the future." In the words of Leonardo Boff, Francis has "put the people of God at the center,"[40] and, therefore, also, the ecclesiological spirit of the Second Vatican Council.

NOTES

1. The future pope entered the Jesuits in 1958, taught at a high school during 1964–65, was ordained priest in 1969, and took final vows as a Jesuit in 1974.

2. Mario I. Aguilar offers a brief overview of the immediate postconciliar atmosphere across Latin America in general in *Pope Francis: His Life and Thought* (Cambridge: Lutterworth, 2014), 22–34. He briefly discusses Bergoglio's formation at 40–42 and 53–48. On the distinctive situation in Argentinian society in general, including Catholicism and the turmoil of the military dictatorship, see also, 59–82. On divisions within the church in

Argentina, particularly among its Jesuits, see Paul Vallely, *Pope Francis: Untying the Knots* (New York: Bloomsbury, 2013), 38–61. CELAM itself moved in an increasingly more conservative and reactionary direction, particularly from 1972 onward.

3. Succinct yet incisive overviews of the key debates concerning the Council include John O'Malley, *What Happened at Vatican II* (Cambridge, MA: Harvard University Press, 2008); and Giuseppe Alberigo, *A Brief History of Vatican II* (Maryknoll, NY: Orbis, 2006).

4. See, for example, O'Malley's treatment of such debates in *What Happened at Vatican II*. As an example of the persective of employing continuity as the hermenuetical key for interpreting Vatican II, see Joseph Ratzinger with Vittorio Messori, *The Ratzinger Report* (San Francisco: Ignatius Press, 1985), 35–38.

5. Homily preached on April 16, 2013; see http://www.news.va/en/news/pope-2nd-vatican-council-work-of-holy-spirit-but-s.

6. Ibid.

7. See Pope Francis, apostolic exhortation, *Evangelii gaudium*, November 24, 2013, no. 37 (citing *Summa Theologica* II-II, q. 30, a. 4), http://w2.vatican.va/content/francesco/en/apost_exhortations/documents/papa-francesco_esortazione-ap_20131124_evangelii-gaudium.html. See, also nos. 3, 24, 43–44, 112, 164, 188, 194, 197–98, 252, 285 and, especially, 114, 179, and 193.

8. Pope John XXIII, *Ad Petri Cathedram*, June 29, 1959, no. 72: "In essentials, unity; in doubtful matters, liberty; in all things, charity."

9. Address delivered on October 11, 1962.

10. "I have chosen not to explore these many questions which call for further reflection and study," no.16.

11. Although one should not downplay the more ambivalent sections of the document and mixed messages contained therein as we have heard from Francis in other contexts.

12. Indeed, while he references John Paul II's *Apostolos suos*, at the very same time, he is in effect, questioning the perspective and limitations upon the authority and remit of episcopal conferences contained in that document (see no. 32).

13. O'Malley, *What Happened at Vatican II*, 191. This suggestion was never followed through during the Council because of developments concerning the synod of bishops.

14. On the notion of "people of God," see Karl Rahner, "People of God," in Karl Rahner, ed., *Encyclopedia of Theology: The Concise Sacramentum Mundi* (New York: Crossroad, 1975), 1204–6.

15. Yves Congar was among the chief architects of this breakthrough and the notion coming to figure so prominently at the Council in general. Congar helped to draft *Lumen gentium* itself. See his Yves Congar, "The Church: The People of God," in *Concilium*, vol. 1 (The Church and Mankind) (New York: Paulist Press, 1965), 12–13.

16. For example, see José Comblin, *People of God* (Maryknoll, New York: 2004); Peter De Mey, "Recent Views of Lumen Gentium: Fifty Years after Vatican II," *Horizons* 39, no. 2 (2012): 252–81.

17. Indeed the Latin American bishops at Vatican II had contributed to many of the key ecclesiological debates, including on this very issue.

18. It was a theme that bridged the sense of the covenant in the Hebrew Bible and the notion of a new covenant with the gentiles also, as developed in the early church. On the ecclesiological shifts marked by Vatican II, see also the chapter by Thomas Rausch in this volume.

19. It is debatable whether it should be termed a metaphor as such, because it can be argued that it truly describes what the church existentially is, rather than drawing upon other, distinct realities to compare to the church.

20. Although a sense of hierarchy remained at Vatican II, including, as noted in *Lumen gentium* itself, especially chap. 3.

21. Comblin, *People of God*, 4–10.

22. In the late 1960s, a group of theologians had formed the "Communio" Program, among whom Ratzinger would prove pivotal. Gradually, the ecclesiological vision of this group would become that of the official church. See, for example, Gerard Mannion, *Ecclesiology and Postmodernity* (Collegeville, MN: Michael Glazier, 2007), 25–101; Joseph Ratzinger, "Communio: A

Program," *Communio: International* Review 19, no. 3 (1992): 436–49. See, also, his critique of the notion of church as people of God in his *Church, Ecumenism and Politics* (Slough, UK: St. Paul, 1988), 14–28.

23. See Peter De Mey, "Recent Views of *Lumen gentium*," esp. 255–57.

24. Matthias Scharer and Jochen Hilberath, *The Practice of Communicative Theology* (New York: Crossroad, 2008), 90–91. These developments culminated in the CDF document of 1990, "*Communionis Notio*."

25. Comblin, *People of God*, 11.

26. See Mannion, *Ecclesiology and Postmodernity*, 75–101.

27. Comblin, *People of God*, 13.

28. He consciously echoes *Lumen gentium* (e.g., no. 9) in reminding us that the church's "ultimate foundation is in the free and gracious initiative of God" (no. 111). *Evangelii gaudium* differs from the 2007 CELAM final document from Aparecida, which also balanced the by then official emphasis on *communio* alongside the notion of people of God but which gave much more prominence to the sense of *communio* throughout, in comparison with *Evangelii gaudium*. Nonetheless, that document clearly also reaffirmed the notion of the people of God, the document as a whole reflecting the tensions between different preferred ecclesiological visions among the CELAM bishops themselves.

29. My emphasis.

30. Note Vatican II's sense of the church as transformative sacrament and also as servant returning.

31. A concept, borrowed from the Lutheran scholar Oscar Cullman, which Bergoglio was employing long before his election to the papacy, see, for example, Francesca Ambrogetti and Sergio Rubin, *Pope Francis: His Life in His Own Words* (New York: G.P. Putnam's Sons, 2013), 227–28.

32. Francis underlines the Vatican II commitment to the vocation of the laity and again challenges a hierarchical vision of the church in no. 102, where he states unambiguously that "lay people are, put simply, the vast majority of the people of God. The minority—ordained ministers—are at their service."

He criticizes "an excessive clericalism which keeps...[the laity] away from decision-making."

33. See, for example, *Evangelii gaudium* 15, 23, 47.

34. John XXIII, "Gaudet Mater Ecclesia," October 11, 1962, http://www.vatican.va/holy_father/john_xxiii/speeches/1962/doc uments/hf_j-xxiii_spe_19621011_opening-council_lt.html.

35. http://www.vatican.va/archive/hist_councils/ii_vatican _council/documents/vat-ii_decree_19641121_unitatis-redintegra tio_en.html.

36. *Evangelii gaudium*, especially nos. 36 and 246. Cf. also *Unitatis redintegratio* 11. This is discussed at greater length in the chapter in this volume by Richard Gaillardetz.

37. See also no. 41, where he cites John Paul II's Encyclical Letter, *Ut unum sint* (May 25, 1995), 19: AAS 87 (1995), 933 on how the expression of truth necessarily takes different forms.

38. Again, consider his admonishment of clericalism, ambition, and careerism.

39. Significantly, Comblin opens his study with the following words: "This book has been written in view of the next papacy. It expresses hope for a return to the principles of Vatican II. Not Vatican III—there can be no Vatican III without first returning to Vatican II. Such a return is not simply to the texts of the council but to its underlying inspiration as found in John XXIII's speeches and especially his inaugural address (October 11, 1962), which increasingly seems to point the way not merely for the council but for future generations of Christians." Comblin, *People of God*, vii.

40. Leonardo Boff, *Francis of Rome and Francis of Assisi* (Maryknoll, NY: Orbis, 2014), 37.

CHAPTER 5

A LISTENING CHURCH

Thomas P. Rausch, SJ

By his own admission, Jorge Mario Bergoglio wasn't always a listener. He has acknowledged the mistakes he made as a very young provincial, appointed to the office at the age of thirty-six. "I did not always do the necessary consultation. And this was not a good thing….I made my decisions abruptly and by myself."[1] But he learned. As Archbishop of Buenos Aires, he had a meeting with his six auxiliary bishops every two weeks, and several times a year, he met with the council of priests. "They asked questions and we opened the floor for discussion. This greatly helped me to make the best decisions."[2] In a 2015 response to questions sent by residents of a shantytown in Buenos Aires, he stressed the importance of listening to others, adding, "Even if you do not agree with them, they always, always give you something or they put you in a situation that forces you to rethink your position, and this enriches you."[3]

From the beginning of his pontificate, he has stressed the importance of consultation and listening. In his famous interview with the pope, Father Antonio Spadaro said, "It is clear that Pope Francis is more used to having conversations than giving lectures."[4] The pope told his interviewer that he had been warned not to consult too much, to decide by himself. But he said consultation was important, not just for himself, but in the official gatherings of the church:

> The consistories [of cardinals], the synods [of bishops] are, for example, important places to make real and active this consultation. We must, however, give them a less rigid form. I do not want token consultations, but real consultations. The consultation group of eight cardinals, this "outsider" advisory group, is not only my decision, but it is the result of the will of the cardinals, as it was expressed in the general congregations before the conclave. And I want to see that this is a real, not ceremonial consultation.[5]

A FRESH RECEPTION OF VATICAN II

But Pope Francis is more than a church leader who prizes consultation. Faithful to the mandate he received at his election, he is seeking to re-receive the Second Vatican Council's vision of a church as a true communion of bishops and faithful. In his famous *Models of the Church*, Avery Dulles characterized the ecclesiology regnant from Vatican I up to Vatican II as an institutional ecclesiology that divided the church into three powers and functions—teaching, sanctifying, and governing—all in the hands of the bishops. This led, in turn, to further distinctions between the church teaching and the church taught, the church sanctifying and church sanctified, the church governing and the church governed.[6] This top-down ecclesiology, one part active, one part passive, came to expression in Pope Pius X's encyclical addressed to the people of France, *Vehementer nos* (1906), which defined the church as a fundamentally unequal society:

> It follows that the Church is essentially an *unequal* society, that is, a society comprising two categories of persons, the Pastors and the flock, those who occupy a rank in the different degrees of the hierarchy and the multitude of

the faithful. So distinct are these categories that with the pastoral body only rests the necessary right and authority for promoting the end of the society and directing all its members towards that end; the one duty of the multitude is to allow themselves to be led, and, like a docile flock, to follow the Pastors. (no. 8)

Vatican II's Dogmatic Constitution on the Church, *Lumen gentium* (LG), changed the basic image of the church from a juridically understood perfect society (*societas perfecta*) to more biblical images of the church as mystery, people of God, and pilgrim church. In chapter 2 on the people of God, it moved beyond Vatican I's bipartite ecclesiology of active and passive members to a vision of the church as a communion of pastors and laity in the Spirit (LG 13). Not just the bishops but all the faithful shared in Christ's threefold office (no. 31). Its collegial theology of authority included the bishops with the pope in the church's governance. It reinterpreted Vatican I by including the bishops in the exercise of the church's charism of infallible teaching (no. 25). And it taught that the faithful also share in the church's infallibility: "The entire body of the faithful, anointed as they are by the Holy One, cannot err in matters of belief. They manifest this special property by means of the whole peoples' supernatural discernment in matters of faith when 'from the Bishops down to the last of the lay faithful' they show universal agreement in matters of faith and morals" (no. 12).

In the third chapter, "On the Hierarchical Structure of the Church and in Particular on the Episcopate," the Council makes the same point, though more indirectly: "The infallibility promised to the Church resides also in the body of Bishops, when that body exercises the supreme magisterium with the successor of Peter. To these definitions the assent of the Church can never be wanting, on account of the activity of that same Holy Spirit, by which the whole flock of Christ is preserved and progresses in unity of faith" (LG 25). In other words, infallibility pertains not only to hierarchical authority. Authority teaches what the church believes; its role is to articulate the *sensus fidelium* or sense of the faithful of the whole church.

In his interview, Father Spadaro had asked the pope how he understood Saint Ignatius's phrase about "thinking with the church." Francis responded by referring to Vatican II's image of the church as the "holy, faithful people of God," his preferred image, saying that the "people itself constitutes a subject." This means the *whole* church, the totality of God's people, that "complex web of relationships that take place in the human community" into which God enters. This is the church that enjoys in the Spirit an *infallibilitas in credendo*. "We should not even think, therefore, that 'thinking with the church' means only thinking with the hierarchy of the church."[7]

All the faithful, considered as a whole, display this infallibility in believing through a supernatural sense of the faith of all the people walking together. "This is what I understand today as the 'thinking with the church' of which St. Ignatius speaks. When the dialogue among the people and the bishops and the pope goes down this road and is genuine, then it is assisted by the Holy Spirit. So this thinking with the church does not concern theologians only."[8] Richard Gaillardetz comments, "Let us not overlook the audacity of this claim. Francis is saying that we can be confident of an assistance of the Holy Spirit to the bishops on the condition that they are open to listening to others. This perspective stands in startling contrast to the almost mechanistic notions of the assistance of the Holy Spirit often invoked by church leaders."[9] This is a church in which pastors and faithful listen to each other, not just the faithful listening to the hierarchy.

In his apostolic exhortation *Evangelii gaudium* (November 24, 2013), Francis refers again to the anointing of the people of God by the Holy Spirit, making it infallible *in credendo*:

> This means that it does not err in faith, even though it
> may not find words to explain that faith. The Spirit

guides it in truth and leads it to salvation. As part of his mysterious love for humanity, God furnishes the totality of the faithful with an instinct of faith—*sensus fidei* —which helps them to discern what is truly of God. The presence of the Spirit gives Christians a certain connaturality with divine realities, and a wisdom which enables them to grasp those realities intuitively, even when they lack the wherewithal to give them precise expression. (no. 119)

In an address to the International Theological Commission a few weeks later, Francis returned to the image of the church as the entire people of God, speaking of the *"sense of the faith"* as a kind of *"spiritual instinct"* that allows the members to "think with the church" (*sentir con la Iglesia*) and discern what conforms to the apostolic faith. But the sense of the faith cannot be reduced to majority opinion in the sociological sense. Therefore, the magisterium must be "attentive to what the Spirit says to the Churches through the authentic manifestations of the *sensus fidelium*," and it needs theologians to develop criteria for discerning those authentic manifestations.[10]

TOWARD A LISTENING CHURCH

What Francis is proposing is an ecclesiology that takes seriously the nature of the church as a true *communio* of the faithful and their pastors in a synergistic relationship, an ecclesiology that calls for a genuine dialogue between pope and bishops, local churches and Rome, pastors and their faithful. And there are a number of indications that he sees his mandate as moving the church in that direction.

For example, in *Evangelii gaudium*, Francis raises the question of a conversion of the papacy, arguing that episcopal conferences can "contribute in many and fruitful ways to the concrete realization of the collegial spirit." Yet he observes that "a juridical status of episcopal conferences which would see them as subjects of specific attributions, including genuine doctrinal authority, has not yet been sufficiently elaborated. Excessive centralization, rather than proving helpful, complicates the Church's life and her missionary outreach" (no. 32). Pope Benedict's approach was different, insisting that episcopal conferences have no magisterial authority, unless unanimous or approved by Rome. Such an understanding of collegiality also concerns church discipline. For example, while Francis does not seem to be against the ordination of married men to meet the shortage of priests, he wants the proposal to come from regional episcopal conferences, not from the pope.[11]

Another example is the request of Cardinal Lorenzo Baldisseri, Secretary General of the synod of bishops, that bishops around the world in preparation for the synod on the family survey their faithful on questions of divorce and remarriage, rules for annulments, children in marriages not recognized by the church, contraception, and how to minister to those in same-sex relations. While the Cardinal's letter was sent to all the bishops of the United States, an accompanying letter from the general secretary of the United States Conference of Catholic Bishops asked them only to provide their own observations.[12] A Vatican report on the survey released on June 26, 2014, found that "many Christians 'have difficulty' accepting church teachings on key issues such as birth control, divorce, homosexuality and cohabitation."[13] This effort to consult the faithful on questions important to their lives was unprecedented. For many it was a sign of hope.

In June 2014, the International Theological Commission published a text titled "*Sensus Fidei* in the Life of the Church," a doctrine Cardinal Walter Kasper says "is very well established in the biblical and theological tradition, but has often been neglected."[14] After reviewing that tradition, the ITC text argues that the faithful "are not merely passive recipients of what the hierarchy teaches and theologians explain; rather, they are living and active subjects within the Church" (no. 67). They play a role in the development of doctrine, sometimes when bishops and theologians have been divided on an issue (no. 72), and in the development of the church's moral teaching (no. 73). From this it follows "that the magisterium needs means by which to consult the faithful" (no. 74). As the *sensus fidelium* is not simply identical with the majority opinion of the baptized, theology needs to provide principles and criteria for discernment (no. 83), echoing what Francis had said in his address to the ITC the previous December. There is also an ecumenical dimension to the *sensus fidei*; the text asks if separated Christians can be understood as participating in the *sensus fidelium* in some manner, answering in the affirmative (no 86).

The ITC document suggests first, that the old distinction between the church teaching (*ecclesia docens*) and the church taught (*ecclesia discens*), where the church teaching was identified exclusively with the hierarchy, is no longer theologically appropriate. Second, it suggests that the Catholic Church might have something to learn from other churches.

Toward the end, the text notes that problems arise when the majority of the faithful remain indifferent to doctrinal or moral decisions of the magisterium or reject them, perhaps from weak faith or an uncritical embrace of contemporary culture. But it also argues significantly that "it may indicate that certain decisions have been taken by those in authority without due consideration of the experience and the *sensus fidei* of the faithful, or without sufficient consultation of the faithful by the magisterium" (no. 123).

One way to gauge the *sensus fidelium* is through a public exchange of views, using institutional instruments such as local councils inclusive of priests and faithful, diocesan synods, or pastoral councils in parishes, though the text stresses that those taking part in these instruments should be in full communion with the church. But some have asked if those who have for different reasons been alienated from the church might also have important things to say. At the end, the text, echoing Pope Francis, says that the *sensus fidei* is closely related to the "*infallibilitas in credendo*," and that the church as a whole is a believing subject.

Finally, in a speech at the Vatican marking the 50th anniversary of the Synod of Bishops, Pope Francis stressed that the Church is "synodal" from top to bottom. He said, "A synodal church is a listening church, knowing that listening 'is more than feeling.' It is a mutual listening in which everyone has something to learn. Faithful people, the College of Bishops, the Bishop of Rome: we are one in listening to others; and all are listening to the Holy Spirit, the 'Spirit of truth' (Jn 14:17), to know what the Spirit 'is saying to the Churches' (Rev 2:7)."

AN EXTRAORDINARY SYNOD

Pope Francis's desire for a listening church was most evident at the October 2014 Extraordinary General Assembly of the Synod of Bishops on the Family. Established by Pope Paul VI shortly after the Second Vatican Council, the synod meets every three or four years to advise the pope on topics of his choosing. There have also been three Extraordinary General Assemblies of the Synod—in 1969 and 1985, and in 2014. Pope John Paul II once referred to the synods, along with ecumenical councils and national or regional episcopal conferences, as "instruments of collegiality."[15] For each assembly of the synod, the world's episcopal conferences choose a certain number of their members to represent them, while the pope names other bishops of his own choosing, up to 15 percent of the total. Often, he also appoints theological experts or representatives of the laity who take part in the discussions of the smaller language groups but do not have a vote.

In spite of initial high hopes, previous synods have been a disappointment. As Michael Fahey has written, "Each new synod attracts less and less attention; the structure of their sessions has become unwieldy, they have become rituals with little practical impact on the life of the Church."[16] Many of the bishops see them as a waste of time. Much of the problem results from the fact that control of the synod assemblies has remained in the hands of the

Vatican. Conservative Curia staffers prepare the *Lineamenta* or text to be discussed and appoint other staffers to collate the synod's work. For example, at the 1987 Synod on the Laity, where four members of the editorial committee belonged to Opus Dei, a number of specific proposals that found considerable support on the floor such as admitting women to those liturgical ministries not requiring ordination, were deleted, or more accurately, formulated in so general a way in the final list of propositions presented to the bishops for their vote that they were no longer specifically mentioned. This meant that the bishops were not allowed to express their opinion on the issues that had been raised.

How different was Pope Francis's Extraordinary Synod on the Family in 2014. The meeting in October was itself extraordinary. As it opened, Francis instructed the more than 180 synod fathers, cardinals, and bishops on the nature of synodality, encouraging them to speak openly and honestly, using the word *parrhesia*, which means "free speech" or "to speak candidly":

> A basic general condition is this: to speak clearly. No one must say: "This can't be said; he will think of me this way or that...." It is necessary to say everything that is felt with parrhesia. After the last Consistory (February 2014), in which there was talk of the family, a Cardinal wrote to me saying: too bad that some Cardinals didn't have the courage to say some things out of respect for the Pope, thinking, perhaps, that the Pope thought something different. This is not good; this is not synodality, because it is necessary to say everything that in the Lord one feels should be said, with human respect, without fear. And, at the same time, one must listen with humility and receive with an open heart what the brothers say. Synodality will be exercised with these two attitudes.

Therefore, I ask you, please, for these attitudes of brothers in the Lord: to speak with parrhesia and to listen with humility.[17]

The pope's encouragement for more honest conversation was certainly heard by the assembled synod fathers. The synod was unlike any other, with transparency, public disagreement, and cardinals and bishops lining up on different sides of issues and some carrying on the debate in the media. Some took issue with a proposal put forward by Cardinal Walter Kasper to find a way to admit some Catholics in second marriages without an annulment to receive Holy Communion. Others saw this as a violation of church doctrine, or objected to the language in the synod's initial report, acknowledging the gifts of homosexuals who looked for a welcoming home in the church and asking if Catholic communities could offer one.[18] Others supported this more pastoral approach.

For many Catholics, what was most significant was that the Extraordinary Synod seemed like an effort on the part of Pope Francis and many of the bishops to reclaim the free discussion of difficult issues that had characterized the Second Vatican Council. Not a rubber stamp of earlier conclusions, it was an honest admission of differences in theology and pastoral practice. The synod represented a transparency not seen since the Council, a true gathering of bishops to work with the pope. In his concluding address, Pope Francis spoke of the synod as a "journey," outlining in blunt language what he saw as the temptations faced by both conservative and progressive members:

> ...a temptation to hostile inflexibility, that is, wanting to close oneself within the written word, (the letter) and not allowing oneself to be surprised by God, by the God of surprises, (the spirit); within the law, within the certitude of what we know and not of what we still need to learn and to achieve. From the time of Christ, it is the temptation of the zealous, of the scrupulous, of

the solicitous and of the so-called—today—"tradition-alists" and also of the intellectuals.

The temptation to a destructive tendency to good-ness [It. *buonismo*], that in the name of a deceptive mercy binds the wounds without first curing them and treating them; that treats the symptoms and not the causes and the roots. It is the temptation of the "do-gooders," of the fearful, and also of the so-called "pro-gressives and liberals."[19]

Controversial as the synod was, it showed a church attempting to discuss difficult issues honestly, and, while remaining faith-ful to its doctrine, attempting to find pastoral ways of reaching out to those who so often felt excluded. Many Catholics saw it as a sign of hope.

CONCLUSION

Pope Francis inherited a church which in many ways had moved away from the vision of the Second Vatican Council. In John O'Malley's words, the doctrine of collegiality, so important to the council's majority, "ended up an abstract teaching without point of entry into the social reality of the church."[20] The church's nonconsultative style of exercising authority has resulted in a growing divide between its faithful and its hierarchical authorities on questions of contraception, marriage and divorce, the role of women in the church, and homosexuality. From the beginning of his pontificate, Francis has sought to reclaim Vatican II's image of the church as the people of God and its neglected teaching on the sense of the faithful.

The pope's description of the people of God as constituting a subject suggests his concern over the significant differences between official church teachings and how the faithful live their lives as revealed by Cardinal Baldisseri's survey. When asked about Saint Ignatius's principle of "thinking with the church," he pointed not to the hierarchy but to the infallibility in matters of belief *of the whole church*, saying this is how he understands Saint Ignatius's principle. Francis cautions that this is not some form of populism, but how the Second Vatican Council understands the *infallibilitas* of all the faithful, the church as the totality of God's people, pastors and people together.[21]

The concerns of Pope Francis are always pastoral. He insists that reality is more important than ideas and has already given signs that he expects something different from what has been Rome's cautious, traditional approach to pastoral problems in the church's life. For example, according to Father Augusto Zampini, a diocesan priest from Greater Buenos Aires, "When you're working in a shanty town, 90 per cent of your congregation are single or divorced. You have to learn to deal with that. Communion for the divorced and remarried is not an issue. Everyone takes Communion."[22]

Reclaiming the notion of the church's *infallibilitas in credendo* suggests that this pope wants to see a church in which the *sensus fidelium* is effectively honored. In other words, he wants a church that listens and is in dialogue. He returned to this theme in a meeting with the members of the ITC on December 5, 2014, stressing the importance of listening: "The theologian is, above all, a believer who listens to the living Word of God and welcomes it into his heart and mind…but he must also humbly listen to what the Spirit tells the Church through the different manifestations of faith lived by the People of God."[23]

The ITC document on the *sensus fidei* in the church's life observed that the magisterium needs means by which to consult the faithful. How might we image those means of consultation? What kinds of institutional structures might be developed? This remains a challenge for the theological community and for the church. For example, could future synods be given a deliberative voice? Could they be expanded to include a more active participation of the laity, perhaps even giving them a vote? Could more members of the laity with pastoral experience or theological education be included on Vatican dicasteries? How can diocesan pastoral synods be made more effective?

The ITC document also affirms that "separated Christians" can be understood as participating in the *sensus fidelium* in some manner, suggesting that the Catholic Church might have something to learn from other churches on these disputed questions (no. 86). A listening church would reflect much more accurately what it means to be "the holy, faithful people of God."

NOTES

1. Pope Francis, "A Big Heart Open to God: The Exclusive Interview with Pope Francis," *America* 209, no. 8 (September 30, 2013): 20, http://www.americamagazine.org/pope-interview.

2. Ibid.

3. Carol Glatz, "Pope Grants Interview about His Safety, Politics, Virtual Relationships," *Catholic News Service* (March 10, 2015), http://www.catholicregister.org/faith/faith-news/item/198 47-pope-grants-interview-about-his-safety-politics-virtual-relationships.

4. Taken from "Interview with Pope Francis" by Father Antonio Spadaro. Cf. https://w2.vatican.va/content/francesco/en /speeches/2013/september/documents/papa-francesco_20130921 _intervista-spadaro.html.

5. Francis, "A Big Heart Open to God," 20.

6. Avery Dulles, *Models of the Church* (Garden City, NY: Doubleday, 1974), 34.

7. Francis, "A Big Heart Open to God," 22; according to Austen Ivereigh, Bergoglio had discovered the early church formula infallible *in credendo* in his reading of Denzinger's *Enchiridion Symbolorum*; see *The Great Reformer: Francis and the Making of a Radical Pope* (New York: Henry Holt, 2014), 111.

8. Francis, "A Big Heart Open to God," 22.

9. Richard R. Gaillardetz, "The Francis Moment: A 'Kairos' for Catholic Ecclesiology," *Proceedings of the Catholic Theological Society of America* 69 (2014): 72.

10. "Address of Pope Francis to the Members of the International Theological Commission," December 6, 2013, http:

//w2.vatican.va/content/francesco/en/speeches/2013/decem
ber/documents/papa-francesco_20131206_commissione-teolog
ica.html.

11. David Gibson, "Are Married Priests Next on Pope
Francis' Reform Agenda," *National Catholic Reporter* (May 9–22,
2014), 12.

12. See http://www.scribd.com/doc/180575701/Vatican-
questionnaire-for-the-synod-on-the-family.

13. Josephine McKenna, "Vatican Confronts Shifting
Landscape on Family Issues," *Religion News Service*, June 26, 2014,
http://www.religionnews.com/2014/06/26/vatican-confronts-
shifting-landscape-on-family-issues/.

14. Walter Kasper, "Open House: How Pope Francis Sees the
Church," *Commonweal* 142, no. 7 (April 10, 2015): 13.

15. *L'Osservatore Romano*, September 17–18, 1979; cited by
Charles M. Murphy, "Collegiality: An Essay toward Better
Understanding," *Theological Studies* 46 (1985): 41.

16. Michael Fahey, "The Synod of America: Reflections of a
Nonparticipant," *Theological Studies* 59 (1998): 489.

17. See http://www.zenit.org/en/articles/synod14-full-text-
of-pope-francis-opening-words.

18. "Relatio post disceptitionem" of the General Rapporteur,
Cardinal Péter Erdö, no. 50, http://press.vatican.va/content/sala
stampa/en/bollettino/pubblico/2014/10/13/0751/03037.html.

19. Vatican Radio (October 10, 2014), http://en.radiovatic
ana.va/news/2014/10/18/pope_francis_speech_at_the_conclu
sion_of_the_synod/1108944.

20. John W. O'Malley, *What Happened at Vatican II?*
(Cambridge, MA: Belknap Press of Harvard University, 2008), 311.

21. Francis, "A Big Heart Open to God," 22.

22. Paul Vallely, "The Crisis that Changed Pope Francis,"
Newsweek, October 23, 2014, http://www.newsweek.com/2014/
10/31/crisis-changed-pope-francis-279303.html; see also Paul
Vallely, *Pope Francis: Untying the Knots* (London: Bloomsbury,
2013), 138.

23. Vatican Information Service 22/217 (December 5, 2104),
visnews_en@mlists. vatican.va.

CHAPTER 6

A DIALOGIC CHURCH

Catherine E. Clifford

Speaking to the leaders of Brazilian society in Rio de Janeiro several months after his election, Pope Francis commented that religious traditions have much to contribute to the constructive dialogue that is so necessary to meeting the challenges of our time. "When leaders in various fields ask me for advice," he said, "my response is always the same: dialogue, dialogue, dialogue." He continued,

> The only way for individuals, families and societies to grow, the only way for the life of peoples to progress, is via the culture of encounter, a culture in which all have something good to give and all can receive something good in return. Others always have something to give me, if we know how to approach them in a spirit of openness and without prejudice. This open spirit, without prejudice, I would describe as "social humility," which is what favours dialogue. Only in this way can understanding grow between cultures and religions, mutual esteem without needless preconceptions, in a climate that is respectful of the rights of everyone. Today, we either take the risk of dialogue, we risk the

culture of encounter, or we all fall; this is the path that will bear fruit.[1]

Pope Francis's conviction regarding the importance and effectiveness of dialogue in human relations, at both the interpersonal and broader social levels, can be seen as an extension of his vision of the church and its mission, a vision largely informed by the ecclesiology of the Second Vatican Council. He has repeatedly called upon Catholics to put their faith at the service of an authentic culture of encounter and modeled the priority of dialogue in word and deed.

In the centuries that preceded the Second Vatican Council (1962–65), the basic stance of Catholicism toward modernity, toward other Christians, non-Christian religions, and movements of atheism was for the most part defensive, confrontational, exclusionary, and at times triumphalist. The unprecedented displacement of peoples provoked by the First and Second World Wars broke down many of the religious frontiers that were once indistinguishable from political and geographic boundaries or the divisions of social class. By the early twentieth century, Catholic leaders began to recognize that one of the unintended consequences of a defensive and inwardly focused church was the reinforcement of division and a basic failure to engage the wider culture and society, especially the growing population of the working classes and the poor.

THE ROOTS OF THE DIALOGIC ENGAGEMENT OF THE CHURCH AT VATICAN II

When Pope John XXIII announced the Second Vatican Council in January of 1959, he was deeply aware that the world had changed, necessitating another response from the church. The principal goals that he set before the bishops at Vatican II (*aggiornamento* or "updating," and the restoration of Christian unity) would elicit a commitment to engage in a new culture of dialogue with modern science and culture, and with contemporary people—one that would take into account the fact of religious pluralism. When John XXIII died in 1963, following the first session of the council, Pope Paul VI carried forward his vision and gave it flesh in a programmatic encyclical letter on the church, *Ecclesiam suam*, published in August of 1964.[2] Remarkably, much of this document is a meditation on the nature and importance of dialogue. It profoundly influenced the teachings of the Second Vatican Council, which present the practice of dialogue as the primary means of carrying out the mission of the church in the modern world.

Pope Paul saw the source and model of the church's dialogue with humanity in the mutual exchange of love among the three divine persons of the Trinity and in the conversation initiated by God with humankind in salvation history. God's Word brings creation into being. God spoke to the people of Israel through the prophets, and speaks a self-revealing Word in the incarnation of the Son, in the power of the Spirit. In this saving dialogue with humankind, we are drawn into "a dialogue of fervent and unselfish love" and friendship with God. Paul VI saw the church as continuing the "dialogue of salvation" begun between God and humankind in the incarnation of the Divine Word, who entered history through the humanity of Jesus.

The church is the community of those who have responded in gratitude to the Word of love spoken in Christ. In this exchange, God takes the initiative, communicating God's very self in a totally unmerited gift of merciful love (cf. 1 John 4:10). Pope Paul observes that in this dialogue with human persons, God does not impose. Rather, God makes an "appeal of love" while respecting utterly the freedom of each hearer to respond or reject the offer of grace (*Ecclesiam suam* 75). Further, he insists, God's dialogue of salvation extends to all persons, without exclusion (cf. Col 3:11).

Pope Paul envisions this dialogue in a series of concentric circles beginning with the inner life of the church itself, and extending outward to dialogue with other Christians, with other religions—including atheists, and to the wider society and culture. In *Ecclesiam suam*, he develops an understanding of dialogue as a self-critical process where the church is constantly reexamining the gap between its self-understanding and the actual image reflected in its life and practice. The church is always ready to undertake a genuine *metanoia* and reform whenever needed to better proclaim the gospel of love. We know from personal experience how genuine encounter and dialogue with others can change us and reveal to us who we are in our deepest selves. The same is true of the church: dialogue and conversion are linked inextricably.

DIALOGUE, DISCERNMENT, AND CONVERSION IN THE CHURCH TODAY

Today, Pope Francis is carrying forward the fundamental insight and commitment to dialogue that is central to Pope Paul VI's teaching and was embraced by the Second Vatican Council. The Council's Pastoral Constitution on the Church in the Modern World, *Gaudium et spes*, recognizes that dialogue within the church follows from the very nature and mission of the people of God. The manner in which all the baptized faithful relate to one another contributes directly to the accomplishment of the church's mission as they become a sign and living example of the culture of encounter that makes dialogue possible in the world (GS 92). *Gaudium et spes* promotes dialogue with all peoples, including those with differing viewpoints (no. 28), so that the church might contribute to the building of a more just society. It recognizes that through this exchange, while the church may bring a word of light and hope, it can also learn and receive from the advance of the sciences and the riches of culture (no. 44). Similarly, the Decree on the Missionary Activity of the Church, *Ad gentes*, acknowledges that the church has much to learn from what God is already accomplishing in the religious and cultural traditions of others (AG 11). Vatican II's Declaration on Non-Christian Religions, *Nostra aetate*, calls for dialogue with other religious communities and collaboration with them in the promotion of common spiritual, moral, and cultural values within contemporary society (NA 2). It urges dialogue with the Jewish community in particular, to deepen our understanding of the shared patrimony of Christianity and Judaism (no. 4). Finally, the Council's Decree on Ecumenism, *Unitatis redintegratio*, adopts a comprehensive commitment to dialogue with other Christian communities in view of reconciliation and the restoration of full visible communion. Echoing Paul VI's dialogical program for the life of the church, *Unitatis redintegratio* envisions dialogue as a process of humble self-examination leading to renewal and reform wherever necessary, so that the church might reflect the light of Christ more faithfully (UR 4, 6).

In his 2013 apostolic exhortation on the Joy of the Gospel, *Evangelii gaudium*, Pope Francis cites Pope Paul VI's discussion of the attitude of humility and commitment to self-correction that is to characterize the church's dialogical engagement in mission (EG 26).[3] Pope Francis calls for a far reaching "pastoral and missionary conversion" of the church in our time (EG 25), a reexamination of attitudes, structures, and church practices and their capacity to effectively proclaim the core of the gospel message. He invites all the baptized faithful of the Catholic Church to consider whether the present form of the church and its policies truly enable it to fulfill its mission to proclaim the love and mercy of God with effect in today's world. Dialogue within the church is an essential component of this discernment.

Evangelii gaudium exhorts bishops to develop the necessary processes and structures for ongoing communal discernment within their local churches. He notes that, in many places, the laity has not yet come to experience true sharing in the mission of the church. Where diocesan or parish pastoral councils and other structures for dialogue have been poorly implemented, the voice of the lay faithful is not heard and their gifts are not received. Pope Francis suggests that in such contexts, pastors cannot reliably discern the true pastoral needs and priorities of those entrusted to their care (EG 33). As he sees it, genuine pastoral discernment can only take place in a mutually supportive community and within the culture of dialogue and encounter that characterizes genuine ecclesial communion. Meeting with the leadership of the Latin American Bishops' Conference in 2013, Pope Francis raised a number of pointed questions relating to the full participation of the laity in the mission of the church:

> Is pastoral discernment a habitual criterion, through the use of Diocesan Councils? Do such Councils and Parish Councils, whether pastoral or financial, provide real opportunities for lay people to participate in pastoral consultation, organization and planning? The good functioning of these Councils is critical. I believe that on this score, we are far behind.
>
> As pastors, bishops and priests, are we conscious and convinced of the mission of the lay faithful and do we give them the freedom to continue discerning, in a way befitting their growth as disciples, the mission which the Lord has entrusted to them? Do we support them and accompany them, overcoming the temptation to manipulate them or infantilize them?[4]

The pastors of the church must be attuned to the *sensus fidelium*, the sense of faith or instinctive capacity of the baptized faithful to recognize and discern the call of the gospel. To accomplish their responsibility for the missional communion of the local churches, Pope Francis calls upon the bishops to develop structures of dialogue and participation—not for the sake of organizational efficiency or expediency, but with "the missionary aspiration of reaching everyone" (EG 31; cf. 33). In his own ministry of service and pastoral discernment, the bishop is one who listens—not only to those who share his views or tell him what he wants to hear. He excludes no one from his concern.

The International Synod of Bishops is an essential instrument of dialogue that brings together bishops who represent the local churches throughout the world. In his leadership of the two synods focused on the Christian family, Pope Francis has shown a desire to see the synod function as a space for genuine dialogue and discernment. As noted in the previous chapter, at the outset of the Extraordinary Synod of October 2014, he indicated that he considers "speaking honestly...with *parrhesia*" (candidly and without holding back) and listening with humility as the fundamental preconditions for the practice of synodality.[5] In planning two successive synodal gatherings to reflect extensively on the same pastoral concern, he is also demonstrating that discernment is a *process*. It takes time for all to be heard. Through the process of honest and transparent dialogue, bishops come to understand more deeply that the pastoral challenges of Christians in one cultural context differ greatly from those experienced by the people of God in another. They come to appreciate the need, in the diversity of today's church, for a differentiated pastoral response and to see the inadequacy of uniform solutions. The exchange of dialogue is essential to fostering the bonds of communion within the diversity of the global Catholic Church.

DIALOGUE WITH OTHERS AND THE PROCLAMATION OF LOVE

In the simple and direct style of his preaching, Pope Francis has demonstrated a clear preference for unvarnished discourse over the formality of official pronouncements couched in theological jargon. His engaging and dialogical approach is evident in repeated efforts to lay out his agenda and respond to questions through extended interviews with journalists, beginning with Antonio Spadaro, the editor of the Italian Jesuit journal *La Civiltà Cattolica*,[6] and including the atheist founder of *La Repubblica*, Eugenio Scalfari.[7] The granting of this kind of "direct access" to the pope by representatives of the media is without precedent. While those with more traditionalist sensibilities consider the practice unbecoming for a man in his office, it can be seen as a canny and deliberate attempt on the part of Pope Francis to engage in a straight-talking conversation with anyone who cares to listen. The interviews consistently reflect the engaging style of a man of dialogue, unwilling to see his message filtered or mediated by the offices of the Roman court. Francis often speaks of the importance of "proximity" in pastoral ministry. His unmediated style is a reflection of that same desire to get as close as he can to his interlocutors, and to use every means to get his message out.

When Scalfari, a nonbeliever, jokingly intimated that his friends feared that Francis might seek to "convert" him, the pope replied, "Proselytism is solemn nonsense, it makes no sense.... This is important: to get to know people, listen, expand the circle of ideas."[8] The term *proselytism* refers to any activity aimed at "converting" others to one's religious views. In interfaith and ecumenical circles, it has a negative connotation, suggesting a less than honest approach—one that preys upon people in subtle ways, often by misrepresenting others' beliefs or applying forms of psychological or moral pressure. "Friendly conversation" and even forms of social outreach can become occasions for subtle coercion and manipulation by unprincipled "evangelizers."[9] Such improper attitudes and behavior in Christian witness fail to respect the dignity and freedom of nonbelievers or those belonging to other religious traditions.

Pope Francis restates his conviction concerning this matter in *Evangelii gaudium*, insisting, "It is not by proselytizing that the Church grows, but 'by attraction'" (EG 14).[10] In doing so, he echoes the Second Vatican Council's embrace of the principle of the freedom of conscience in religious matters, grounded in the utmost respect for the freedom of every human person created in the image and likeness of God. In the conciliar period, ecumenical leaders were adamant that without adhesion to this basic principle, the Catholic Church's commitment to dialogue with others might be viewed as an empty promise.[11] Vatican II set the church on course for dialogue in a spirit of openness and mutual trust, of friendship, respect, and service. Francis's views on this question are consistent with the Second Vatican Council's Declaration on Religious

Freedom, *Dignitatis humanae*, which presents dialogue as a common search for the truth, while eschewing the effort to convert others to one's point of view (DH 3). Genuine dialogue requires confidence in the persuasive force of truth and the humility to learn from others. *Dignitatis humanae* observes that the church's respect for the freedom of all persons is rooted in the divine pedagogy reflected in Jesus' own proclamation of the gospel (no. 11).

Pope Francis reiterates this teaching when he asserts that the mission of the church is not proselytism, but love. In conversation with Eugenio Scalfari, he observes, "Our goal is not to proselytize but to listen to needs, desires and disappointments, despair, hope. We must restore hope to young people, help the old, be open to the future, spread love. Be poor among the poor. We need to include the excluded and preach peace."[12] His words resonate with Pope Paul's vision of the church's relationship with the world and with the opening lines of Vatican II's Pastoral Constitution on the Church in the Modern World: "The joys and hopes, the grief and anguish of the people of our time, especially those who are poor or afflicted, are the joys and hopes, the grief and anguish of the followers of Christ" (GS 1). That document calls all the Catholic faithful to establish a dialogue with the world and with people "of all shades of opinion" (no. 43). It presents "sincere and prudent dialogue" as the key to "the rightful betterment of this world in which all alike live" (no. 21).

In his apostolic exhortation *Evangelii gaudium*, Pope Francis sketches out three key areas for the dialogical engagement of the church, namely: social, interreligious, and ecumenical relations.

SOCIAL DIALOGUE

When writing on social dialogue, Pope Francis refers to the conversation between church and society—including political institutions, culture, and contemporary science—at the service of peace and the common good. The church engages in social dialogue in order to promote the full and integral development of human persons and of the social order. On the national and international stage, the church proclaims the "gospel of Peace" (Eph 6:15) and works to promote "a just, responsive, and inclusive society" through dialogue (EG 239). Pope Francis has encouraged such conversation through his prophetic visits to the Italian island of Lampedusa, a landing point for waves of anxious refugees who cross the Mediterranean in a desperate flight from the violence and poverty of fragile states in Africa and the Middle East, often at the hands of unscrupulous human traffickers. In his 2014 pilgrimage to the Holy Land, Pope Francis, together with the Ecumenical Patriarch Bartholomew I of Constantinople, was moved to invite the President of Israel, Shimon Perez, and his Palestinian counterpart, Mahmoud Abbas, to plant an olive tree in the gardens of the Vatican City. This symbolic gesture, supported by common prayer, was intended to encourage perseverance in the efforts of dialogue and reconciliation in the pursuit of peace.

Pope Francis has spoken often of the need to overcome the tyranny of an economic system that enriches a privileged few and neglects the needs of the poor (EG 53–60). Critical of a "disposable" culture that disvalues and excludes the elderly and the poor, he recalls the dignity of all and the need to build a more inclusive society (EG 186–92). While affirming the responsibility of the church to propose the values of human dignity and the common good, Francis suggests that its interventions must be tempered with "profound social humility," mindful that "in her dialogue with the State and with society, the church does not have solutions for every particular issue" (EG 240–41). The church proposes guiding values, while also learning through its dialogue with contemporary science and culture.

INTERRELIGIOUS DIALOGUE

Echoing the teaching of his predecessors, Pope Francis maintains that there is an inseparable connection between dialogue and proclamation in relations with non-Christians (EG 251). He contends, "Interreligious dialogue and evangelization do not exclude one another, but nourish one another mutually."[13] He sees dialogue as a form of witness, a way in which the church respectfully walks alongside others, in the hope that they, too, might encounter Christ. Genuine dialogue, far from compromising one's identity or leading to relativism, sharpens self-awareness. "True openness involves remaining steadfast in one's deepest convictions, clear and joyful in one's own identity, while at the same time being 'open to understanding those of the other party' and 'knowing that dialogue can enrich each side'" (EG 251).[14] We enter into dialogue without ulterior motive, ready to learn and receive from others. "We do not impose anything, we do not employ any subtle strategies for attracting believers; rather, we bear witness to what we believe and who we are with joy and simplicity."[15] In Jesus, who spoke simply and from the heart with those around him, radiating joy as he did so, he finds the model for all those who are called to communicate the good news (EG 141–44).

Pope Francis emphasizes the special bond that joins the church to the Jewish people, insisting that Christians "cannot consider Judaism a foreign religion" (EG 247). Because of Christianity's dependence on the Jewish faith and the shared patrimony of these two traditions, he urges that "dialogue and friendship with the children of Israel are part of the life of Jesus' disciples" (EG 248). Francis knows from experience that the complementarity of Christianity and Judaism "allows us to read the texts of the Hebrew Scriptures together and to help one another to mine the riches of God's word" (EG 249). During the years of his ministry as Archbishop of Buenos Aires, he developed strong personal ties with the Jewish community. With Rabbi Abraham Skorka, then Cardinal Bergoglio co-authored a book that testifies to their deep and wide-ranging experience of dialogue.[16] These encounters sensitized Pope Francis to the need to continue the struggle against the persecution of the Jews and to the possibilities of cooperation in the service of the common good on the basis of shared religious values.

During his visit to Turkey in November 2014, Pope Francis demonstrated his commitment to dialogue with Islam, stopping to pray in Istanbul's historic Blue Mosque. He has called upon all Christians to "avoid hateful generalizations" when faced with the presence of fundamentalism and distortions of the Islamic tradition in the world today (EG 253). In January 2015, he met with the leaders of Buddhist, Hindu, Muslim, and Christian communities in Sri Lanka, where he urged the pursuit of interreligious dialogue to foster healing and unity, and to mend the wounds inflicted by civil strife.[17]

ECUMENICAL DIALOGUE

Dialogue is a mutual exchange that demands humility and listening on the part of the followers of Christ. This is especially true in the experience of dialogue with other Christians, where ecumenical partners seek a deeper and fuller understanding of their common faith in Christ. The Second Vatican Council's Decree on Ecumenism explicitly links the process of dialogue with other Christians to Catholic responsibility for continual self-examination and ongoing reform (UR 4, 6–7). The Council did not hesitate to recognize that at times, other Christian communities have arrived at a deeper insight or better expressed some aspect of our common tradition of faith. In such cases, it affirms, "these various theological expressions are to be considered often as mutually complementary rather than conflicting" (no. 17). Their insights can enrich our own understanding of the gospel.

In his message for World Communications Day 2014, Pope Francis wrote, "To dialogue means to believe that the 'other' has something worthwhile to say, and to entertain his or her point of view and perspective. Engaging in dialogue does not mean renouncing our own ideas and traditions, but the claim that they alone are valid or absolute."[18] In more pointed language, he develops a similar line of reflection when speaking of ecumenical relations: "How many important things unite us! If we really believe in the abundantly free working of the Holy Spirit, we can learn so much from one another! It is not just about being better informed about others, but rather about reaping what the Spirit has sown in them, which is also meant to be a gift for us" (EG 246).

Pope Francis seems deeply aware that dialogue between theologians cannot suffice to resolve all that divides the churches and, leading by way of example, he has made the ecumenism of life a high priority. He has consistently worked together with the leaders of other Christian churches to promote initiatives for common witness and common prayer. In March 2014, Pope Francis and Archbishop Justin Welby of Canterbury concluded a joint agreement to support the work of the Global Freedom Network, a groundbreaking initiative in the fight against modern-day slavery and human trafficking.[19] In May 2014, he traveled to Jerusalem with the Ecumenical Patriarch Bartholomew I, leader of the Eastern Orthodox Churches, to commemorate the historic exchange of peace between Pope Paul VI and Ecumenical Patriarch Athenagoras I in that city fifty years earlier. That historic encounter led to the lifting of the mutual excommunications of 1054 at the close of the Second Vatican Council, and prepared the way for the inauguration of official dialogue between the Catholic and Orthodox Churches. Meeting with a delegation of the Evangelical Lutheran Church in December 2014, Pope Francis spoke of the forthcoming commemoration of the Lutheran Reformation in 2017, which Catholics and Lutherans can mark together, thanks to fifty years of sustained dialogue:

> On that occasion, Lutherans and Catholics around the world will, for the first time, have the opportunity to share the same ecumenical commemoration, not in the form of a triumphalistic celebration, but as the profession of our common faith in the Triune God. At the center of this event, therefore, there will be common prayer and the plea that our Lord Jesus Christ pardon

for our mutual faults, along with the joy of journeying together on a shared ecumenical path.[20]

While serving as Archbishop of Buenos Aires, Jorge Bergoglio developed friendships with Pentecostal leaders, who represent the fastest growing movement within global Christianity today. In his ministry as Bishop of Rome, Pope Francis has continued to reach out to Evangelical and Pentecostal communities. In July 2014, he traveled to the town of Caserta in Southern Italy to meet with Evangelical and Pentecostal leaders. At that gathering, he asked forgiveness for the times when members of the Catholic Church had failed to recognize them as brothers and sisters in Christ.[21]

CONCLUSION

In all of these activities that touch upon social, interreligious, and ecumenical dialogue, Pope Francis models the kind of initiative and dialogical engagement that he considers desirable at every level of Catholic ecclesial life. Beginning with the conclave that preceded his election and throughout his pontificate, Francis has decried a church that is inward-looking and self-referential. An evangelizing church, one capable of proclaiming the merciful love of God in faith, must be prepared to go out to the peripheries, to encounter others in dialogue. As his many words and deeds make clear, this is the principal means of the church's discernment and missional engagement. To become the dialogic church that Pope Francis envisions will require a concerted investment in the formation of adult Christians versed in the habits of dialogue, men and women who "know how to enter bravely into the Areopagus of contemporary cultures and to initiate dialogue."[22]

NOTES

1. Pope Francis, "Meeting with Brazil's Leaders of Society," Rio di Janeiro, July 27, 2013, http://w2.vatican.va/content/frances

co/en/speeches/2013/july/documents/papa-francesco_201307 27_gmg-classe-dirigente-rio.html.

2. Paul VI, *Ecclesiam suam*, Encyclical On the Church, August 6, 1964, http://w2.vatican.va/content/paul-vi/en/encycli cals/documents/hf_p-vi_enc_06081964_ecclesiam.html.

3. Pope Francis, Apostolic Exhortation on the Joy of the Gospel: On the Proclamation of the Gospel in Today's World, *Evangelii gaudium*, http://w2.vatican.va/content/francesco/en/ apost_exhortations/documents/papa-francesco_esortazione-ap_20131124_evangelii-gaudium.html. Citing *Ecclesiam suam*, nos. 9–11. All subsequent references to *Evangelii gaudium* are taken from this version and will be indicated by the abbreviation "EG" in parentheses, in the body of the text.

4. Pope Francis, "Address to the Leadership of the Episcopal Conferences of Latin America during the General Coordination Meeting," July 28, 2013, http://w2.vatican.va/content/francesco /en/speeches/2013/july/documents/papa-francesco_201307 28_gmg-celam-rio.html.

5. Pope Francis, "Greeting to the Synod Fathers during the First Congregation of the Third Extraordinary General Assembly of the Synod of Bishops," October 6, 2014, http://w2.vatican.va/ content/francesco/en/speeches/2014/october/documents/papa-francesco_20141006_padri-sinodali.html.

6. Antonio Spadaro, "A Big Heart Open to God," *America*, September 30, 2013, http://americamagazine.org/pope-interview.

7. Eugenio Scalfari, "The Pope: How the Church will Change," *La Repubblica*, October 1, 2013, http://www.repubblica. it/cultura/2013/10/01/news/pope_s_conversation_with_scalfari _english-67643118/.

8. Ibid.

9. The topic of proselytism has been an important theme of study in ecumenical relations. For an important recent perspective, see World Council of Churches, Pontifical Council for Interreligious Dialogue, World Evangelical Alliance, "Christian Witness in a Multi-religious World: Recommendations for Conduct," June 28, 2011, http://www.oikoumene.org/en/resources /documents/wcc-programmes/interreligious-dialogue-and-coop

eration/christian-identity-in-pluralistic-societies/christian-wit
ness-in-a-multi-religious-world.

10. Here Pope Francis cites a homily delivered by Pope
Benedict XVI during the meeting of the Latin American Bishops'
Conference at Aparecida, "Homily at Mass for the Opening of the
Fifth General Conference of the Latin American and Caribbean
Bishops (May 13, 2007), Aparecida, Brazil," *AAS* 99 (2007): 437.

11. For more extensive information on the ecumenical significance of the Decree on Religious Liberty, see Catherine E.
Clifford, "The Ecumenical Context of *Dignitatis Humanae*: Forty
Years After Vatican II," *Science et Esprit* 59, nos. 2–3 (2007):
387–403.

12. Scalfari, "The Pope: How the Church Will Change."

13. Pope Francis, "Address to Plenary Assembly of the
Pontifical Council for Interreligious Dialogue," November 28,
2013, http://w2.vatican.va/content/francesco/en/speeches/2013/
november/documents/papa-francesco_20131128_pc-dialogo-
interreligioso.html.

14. Cf. John Paul II, encyclical, *Redemptoris missio*, December
7, 1990, no. 56: *AAS* 83 (1991): 304.

15. Pope Francis, "Address to Plenary Assembly of the
Pontifical Council for Interreligious Dialogue," November 28,
2013.

16. Jorge Mario Bergoglio and Abraham Skorka, *On Heaven
and Earth* (New York: Random House, 2013); Original version:
Sobre el cielo y la tierra (Random House Mondadori, S.A., 2010).

17. Pope Francis, "Address of His Holiness Pope Francis:
Interreligious and Ecumenical Gathering," Colombo, January 13,
2015, http://w2.vatican.va/content/francesco/en/speeches/2015
/january/documents/papa-francesco_20150113_srilanka-filip
pine-incontro-interreligioso.html.

18. Pope Francis, "Message of Pope Francis for the 48th
World Communications Day: Communications at the Service of
an Authentic Culture of Encounter," June 1, 2014, http://w2.vatican
.va/content/francesco/en/messages/communications/documents
/papa-francesco_20140124_messaggio-comunicazioni-sociali
.html.

19. "New Initiatives by Global Faiths to Eradicate Modern Slavery and Human Trafficking by 2020," March 17, 2014, http://anglicancentre.churchinsight.com/Articles/396314/Anglican _Centre_in/Justice_and_Peace/GLOBAL_FREEDOM_NET WORK/Global_Freedom_Network.aspx.

20. Pope Francis, "Address of His Holiness Pope Francis to a Delegation from the Evangelical Lutheran Church of Germany," December 18, 2014, http://w2.vatican.va/content/francesco/en/ speeches/2014/december/documents/papa-francesco_2014 1218_chiesa-evangelica-luterana.html.

21. Pope Francis, "Address: Pentecostal Church of Reconciliation, Caserta," July 28, 2014, http://w2.vatican.va/con tent/francesco/en/speeches/2014/july/documents/papa-frances co_20140728_caserta-pastore-traettino.html.

22. Pope Francis, "Address to Participants at the Plenary Session of the Congregation for Catholic Education," February 13, 2014, https://w2.vatican.va/content/francesco/en/speeches/ 2014/february/documents/papa-francesco_20140213_congre gazione-educazione-cattolica.html.

CHAPTER 7

THE LOCAL AND UNIVERSAL CHURCH

Christopher Ruddy

"It seems that my brother Cardinals have gone to the ends of the earth to get [a new pope]…but here we are….I thank you for your welcome. The diocesan community of Rome now has its Bishop." With these words from the central balcony of Saint Peter's Basilica, the newly elected Pope Francis began his greetings to the church and the world. In a pontificate in which his every comment and deed seems programmatic, these few words were surely neither accidental nor incidental. They indicated a distinctive vision of the church and of the papacy, one that has come into clearer focus over the past two years. Furthermore, the election of a pope from the southern hemisphere, a pope who is a religious and lacking in curial experience—and who is therefore literally "eccentric"—is in itself an unmistakable statement about the relationship of the local churches and the universal church in Catholicism.

That relationship has been the subject of much discussion and controversy in recent decades, especially after the Second Vatican Council. One need recall only the very public exchange in the late 1990s and early 2000s between Cardinal Walter Kasper and the then-Cardinal Joseph Ratzinger.[1] The writings of Andrew

Walls, Lamin Sanneh, and Philip Jenkins, among others, have likewise underscored the theological and ecclesiological ramifications of the profound demographic shifts taking place as contemporary Christianity's center of gravity moves from the northern hemisphere to the southern. Those concerns—for example, about unity and diversity, primacy and collegiality, centralization and subsidiarity, the relationship of church and culture—will only grow in importance in the coming decades and centuries.

Here, we explore Pope Francis's understanding of the relationship between the local and the universal church. That understanding is centered on his distinctive conception of the relationship between the center and the peripheries, the local and the global, the primatial and the collegial-synodal. He has not (yet) left as extensive a body of magisterial-theological reflection on the relationship of the local and universal churches as have his two immediate predecessors, Popes Saint John Paul II and Benedict XVI. But, one might say, echoing Yves Congar's reflections on the death of Pope Saint John XXIII, Francis works by way of "intuitions" rather than "expositions."[2] His writings have an obvious consistency and depth, but his acts and gestures are at least as important as his words.

First, we will examine some basic contexts and concerns that shape his thought on the relationship between the local and universal church; second, we will consider key deeds and symbols that instantiate that vision; third, we will evaluate his thought and practice, and then conclude with a brief reflection on the inseparability of structural and spiritual reforms.

CONTEXT

The first "context" for Pope Francis's conception of the relationship of the local and universal church is the relationship of the center and the peripheries. His preconclave call for the church to go out to the peripheries—geographical ones, certainly, but especially existential ones of "the mystery of sin, of pain, of injustice, of ignorance and indifference to religion, of intellectual currents, and of all misery"[3]—is well-known and programmatic for his pontificate. He sees these peripheries as the privileged places of encounter with Christ and with his people. Ecclesiologically, Francis speaks in *Evangelii gaudium* (The Joy of the Gospel)—the *magna carta* of his pontificate—of the "need to promote a sound 'de-centralization'" (no. 16) in the church, as well as to avoid an "excessive centralization" (no. 32) that hinders the church's life and mission.

On a still deeper level, according to the pope, the de-centering involved in going to the peripheries coincides with the need for the church and believers to be re-centered on Christ. In his preconclave intervention, he famously spoke of a Church wounded by "self-referentiality and a kind of theological narcissism."[4] The remedy to such self-centeredness is to be re-centered on Christ. Speaking to the leaders of the Latin American Episcopal Conferences (CELAM) during World Youth Day in 2013, Francis said,

> That is why I like saying that the position of missionary disciples is not in the center but at the periphery: They live poised towards the peripheries…including the peripheries of eternity, in the encounter with Jesus Christ. In the preaching of the Gospel, to speak of "existential peripheries" decentralizes things; as a rule, we are afraid to leave the center. The missionary disciple is someone "off center": the center is Jesus Christ, who calls us and sends us forth. The disciple is sent to the existential peripheries.[5]

The pope spoke similarly at the February 2015 consistory to the new (as well as more senior) cardinals, noting that the self-centered person "inevitably seeks his own interests," whereas charity "makes us draw back from the center in order to set ourselves in the real center, which is Christ alone."[6] The existential peripheries are the places where Christ the center is found.

Second, *Evangelii gaudium* addresses the relationship of the local and the global. The pope notes extremes to be avoided: an

abstract globalization given over to homogenization and a local-
ism that mummifies into a ghettoized "museum of local folklore"
closed to anything new (no. 234). He seeks, instead, their harmony and mutual enrichment: attentiveness to the "global" helps
one "avoid narrowness and banality," and concern for the "local"
"keeps our feet on the ground" (no. 234). Francis illustrates this
point through his contrast of the "sphere" and the "polyhedron."
The former is "no greater than its parts, where every point is equi-
distant from the center, and there are no differences between
them," while the latter "reflects the convergence of all its parts,
each of which preserves its distinctiveness" (no. 236). The polyhedron thus offers a model for unity in diversity, for recognition
of the worth of locality in a globalizing world and of globality in
a world tempted to factionalism and narcissism.[7]

Third, it is universally acknowledged that the future pope
played a decisive role (as chair of the drafting committee) in the
composition of the concluding document of the fifth general conference in 2007 of the Conference of Latin American and Caribbean
Bishops (CELAM) in Aparecida, Brazil. This Aparecida document is
characterized above all by its emphasis on the church as a community of missionary disciples. Speaking as pope to the Latin
American bishops in Aparecida on the occasion of his trip to the
2013 World Youth Day, he noted some hallmarks of that document's genesis: its inductive, dialogical process of composition; the
generative role of popular piety and prayer, as the bishops met
together at Aparecida's Marian shrine; and its emphasis on ecclesial
mission.[8] Richard Gaillardetz has noted that Francis's ecclesiological vision emphasizes mission more strongly than communion
(although it in no way denies the church's communional nature);
it is "centrifugal" rather than "centripetal."[9] Francis's ecclesiology is
mission-centered from beginning to end, and so it is not surprising
that he views the relationship of the local churches and the universal church through the lens and finality of mission.

In each of these ways, therefore, the pope revises and even
reverses the spatial imagery of the center and the periphery: the

church's center is found, paradoxically, in its peripheries. The church comes to itself by going out.

DEEDS, INSTITUTIONS, AND SYMBOLS

Pope Francis's overall vision of the relationship between the local and the universal has taken shape in various key decisions and orientations. First, there is his use of "Bishop of Rome" and "Church of Rome." He is not the first pope to use such titles, of course, but he has given them unprecedented prominence and even centrality. For instance, *Misericordiae vultus* ("Face of Mercy"), the papal bull announcing the "Extraordinary Jubilee" of Mercy, lists simply two papal titles: "Bishop of Rome" and "Servant of the Servants of God." And, as Bishop of Rome, he is the head of the Church of Rome, which "presides in charity," in the words of Saint Ignatius of Antioch that he cited in his first papal speech (and in numerous other addresses since then). Moreover, in a gesture that was more than mere show, he broke with conclave protocol and insisted that the Vicar General for Rome, Agostino Cardinal Vallini, accompany him onto the balcony for his first papal blessing. Francis literally and symbolically put the local Church of Rome front and center at the beginning of his pontificate.

Furthermore, it must also be noted that the pope has joined this terminological and symbolic conversion to a blunt assessment of the need for a reform of the papacy itself:

> Since I am called to put into practice what I ask of others, I too must think about a conversion of the papacy. It is my duty, as the Bishop of Rome, to be open to suggestions which can help make the exercise of my ministry more faithful to the meaning which Jesus Christ wished to give it and to the present needs of evangelization. Pope John Paul II asked for help in finding "a way of exercising the primacy which, while in no way renouncing what is essential to its mission, is

nonetheless open to a new situation." We have made little progress in this regard. The papacy and the central structures of the universal Church also need to hear the call to pastoral conversion. (EG 32)

Second, Francis's decision to create a "Council of Eight [now Nine]" cardinals, comprised almost entirely of residential (and noncurial) bishops from each of the inhabited continents, is perhaps the most concrete expression of his intent to strengthen the role of the local churches in the governance of the universal church. It is not coincidental, either, that many of the members of the C9 are present or former presidents of their national or regional episcopal conferences. The C9 thus has the potential to advance significant curial reform, as well as to register the voices of the local churches around the globe.[10]

Third, Francis has signaled his desire to revalorize the role of episcopal conferences. *Evangelii gaudium* notes,

The Second Vatican Council stated that, like the ancient patriarchal Churches, episcopal conferences are in a position "to contribute in many and fruitful ways to the concrete realization of the collegial spirit." Yet this desire has not been fully realized, since a juridical status of episcopal conferences which would see them as subjects of specific attributions, including genuine doctrinal authority, has not yet been sufficiently elaborated. Excessive centralization, rather than proving helpful, complicates the Church's life and her missionary outreach. (no. 32)

Perhaps most significant in this regard is his willingness to revisit the question of the teaching authority of episcopal conferences. He cites John Paul II's 1998 apostolic letter, *Apostolos suos*, which placed strict limits on such authority, only to suggest that their magisterial authority "has not yet been sufficiently elaborated." Such phrasing is a diplomatic way of calling for change.

Francis's desire to revitalize episcopal conferences can be seen also in two seemingly insignificant details. Seventeen footnotes in *Evangelii gaudium* refer to various documents of national and regional episcopal conferences (Latin America and the Caribbean, United States, France, Brazil, Philippines, Congo, India; note the diversity of continents); he thus has indicated his desire to unite their teaching authority to his. This citing of the concerns of other episcopal conferences is even more true of his encyclical on care for the earth, *Laudato si'* (2015). His concern for episcopal conferences and their collegial nature finds further expression in his change of protocol for the bishops' *ad limina* visits (trips to Rome made roughly every five years by the bishops of a given nation or region to report on the state of their dioceses): he simply distributes to the gathered bishops the text of his prepared remarks, preferring instead to engage with them in open dialogue; such a practice fosters, in a small but real way, a climate of brotherhood and collegiality.

Fourth, Francis's commitment to revitalizing the international synod of bishops is a response to decades of criticism that these synods have been too tightly controlled in their scope and in their procedures. Even though Pope Benedict XVI, in response to such criticisms, had earlier instituted an hour of free discussion at the end of each day of the synods, the Extraordinary Synod in October 2014 manifested an unprecedented level of exchange, engagement, and even significant disagreement. Similarly, the precedence given at the 2014 consistory for the creation of new cardinals to the Secretary General of the Synod of Bishops over the Prefect of the Congregation of the Doctrine of the Faith heralds an ecclesiological shift in balance from the Curia to the local churches.

Fifth, his creation of cardinals is perhaps the most striking, visible sign of his understanding of the local-universal relationship. Several characteristics have emerged from his two cardinalatial consistories. First, the new cardinals come from the geographical peripheries vis-à-vis Rome and the Western world: nine of the sixteen new cardinal-electors at the 2014 consistory, and ten of the fifteen new cardinal-electors at the 2015 consistory. In addition, some "peripheral" countries received their first cardinals: for example, Cape Verde, Myanmar, and Tonga. Second, the new cardinals are overwhelmingly residential-diocesan rather than curial: fifteen out of nineteen at the February 2014 consistory, seventeen out of twenty at the 2015 consistory. Third, even some "Western" cardinals come from noncustomary or "less-influential" sees (for example, in Italy, Perugia and Agrigento instead of Turin and Venice). The pope signaled this preference for the peripheries and their local churches in his homily at the Mass that he celebrated with the new cardinals on February 15, 2015. Reflecting on the Gospel of Mark's account of Jesus' healing of a leper, he directly addressed the new cardinals:

> This is the "logic," the mind of Jesus, and this is the way of the Church. Not only to welcome and reinstate with evangelical courage all those who knock at our door, but to go out and seek, fearlessly and without prejudice, those who are distant, freely sharing what we ourselves freely received.[11]

Finally, the pope has recently decided that newly installed metropolitan archbishops are to receive the pallium (the woolen, cross-embroidered yoke worn during liturgies around the neck and shoulders as a symbol of the shepherd's "burden" of pastoral leadership) in their local churches rather than in Rome. This is a very symbolic gesture, but one with import: Francis is breaking with a thirty-two–year tradition established in 1983 by John Paul II that each metropolitan archbishop is to receive the pallium from the pope at Saint Peter's Basilica on June 29, the solemnity of Saints Peter and Paul. The movement here is from Rome back to the local churches. Monsignor Guido Marini, the Papal Master of Liturgical Ceremonies, said that this change would "better highlight the relationship of the metropolitan archbishops with their local churches, giving more faithful the possibility of being present for this significant rite."[12] The new practice, Marini continued, would also contribute to "that journey of synodality in the Catholic Church which, from the beginning of his pontificate, [Francis] has constantly emphasized as particularly urgent and precious at this time in the history of the Church."[13]

EVALUATION

There is much to commend in Pope Francis's revisioning of the relationship of the local churches and the universal church. In the first place, his personal and ecclesial experience of the "peripheries"—geographic and existential—is decisively important. He has lived in his flesh the relationship of the local and the universal in a way that overcomes what might otherwise remain merely abstract and notional.

Second, he has grasped the importance of fostering a greater sense of episcopal collegiality, not as a check to papal primacy, but as its complement. The full reception of the Second Vatican Council's teaching on collegiality still lies ahead. That relationship must not be seen as a zero-sum game, but as mutually enriching and empowering. A fuller reception of the Council's teaching would also have significant ecumenical implications, particularly with the Orthodox and Eastern Orthodox Churches.

Third, the pope has taken quite seriously the preconclave calls for reform of the Roman Curia. The late French Dominican theologian and ecumenist, Jean-Marie Tillard, noted that it is a perennial—and destructive—temptation to make the Curia a "scapegoat" for all that ails the church.[14] The cardinals who gathered at the conclave of 2013 were nonetheless overwhelmingly agreed that substantial curial reform was needed. It is too early to gauge the long-term effectiveness of Francis's reforming efforts, but he has already made encouraging progress in reforming the Vatican's finances.

His Ignatian spiritual heritage, moreover, fosters a needed climate of discernment and freedom.[15] Here, possibly, is one way that his status as a member of a religious order may make a substantial ecclesiological contribution. The Benedictine and Dominican traditions, for example, can contribute through their respective emphases on broad consultation and on democratic-participatory governance. Although Jesuit governance is sometimes depicted as authoritarian and top-down (for example, provincial leaders are appointed by the Father General, not elected; the "fourth vow" of obedience to the pope, in respect to the missions), Ignatian spirituality also manifests a profound concern for discernment and a deep respect for human freedom. When Pope Francis spoke of his abhorrence to "interfere" in someone's spiritual life, for instance, he likely did not mean a spiritual indifferentism but rather attempts—even well-intentioned—to influence unduly another's discernment and growth.[16]

This spiritual discipline of "noninterference" can be extended ecclesiologically. Ignatian spirituality dwells at the intersection of two of Saint Ignatius's most famous injunctions: to "let the Creator deal directly with the creature" and "to think with the Church"; it is at once deeply personal and radically ecclesial. It is realistic and sober (witness Francis's frequent talk of the devil and the evil spirit). It is capable of accepting uncertainty and of resisting premature closure.[17] It unfolds in a rhetoric of "edification and congratulation," breathing confidence and consolation.[18] It trusts that God is always laboring in his creation to bring it to fulfillment. The pope's Ignatian spirituality may thus be able to make a significant contribution to improving relationships within the churches and the church as a whole.[19]

These "lights" are accompanied, though, by "shadows." One hopes that future synods will continue to develop in a more open, transparent manner. At the Asian synod in 1998, for instance, participants were forbidden to use certain words, such as *subsidiarity*, and other words and themes emphasized by the bishops disappeared in the propositions and final report; similar actions took place at other synods.[20] It is to be "devoutly hoped," as it is said, that the Ordinary Synod of 2015 be more transparent in its conduct and communication. The Extraordinary Synod of 2014 was marked, I hold, by a mix of transparency and opacity. The pope exhorted the synodal participants to *parrhesia*, to bold speech and humble listening.[21] Media reports and commentary are agreed that a wide range of views were expressed. That is a genuine, and much-needed, advance.

And, yet, there were also troubling reports about the control and even manipulation of the Extraordinary Synod: the refusal, for instance, to publish the texts of the participants' interventions or even to provide a substantial summary of them, in favor of vague, anodyne reports from the Vatican Press Office; the opaque preparation of the *relatio post disceptationem* (the midterm summary of the synod, which, in this instance, caused controversy over its comments on nonmarital sexuality and appropriate pastoral responses); and the immediate pushback to the initial refusal by the synod's Secretary General to release the reports of the "small circles"—wherein the participants gather by language-groups to discuss the first week's interventions—reports that were often highly critical of several points in the *relatio post disceptationem*. These defects are easily remediable, but they raise questions about the integrity of the synodal process, and should have been avoided in the first place.[22]

A second, more subtle shadow is the ever-present danger in Catholicism of making the pope "more than a pope," to borrow Jean-Marie Tillard's phrase.[23] The modern and contemporary eras have seen the growth of a centralizing papacy and at times an attendant cult of personality.[24] In the teaching of both Vatican Councils, the pope is certainly the "perpetual and visible principle and foundation for the unity of faith and communion" (*Lumen gentium* 18). And, yet, "the irony," in the words of a Vatican-based Jesuit, "is that this pope, great agent of decentralization in the Church, is personally the most centralized pope since Pius the Ninth. Everything has to cross his desk."[25]

That anonymous quote must be taken with at least a grain of salt, but it is striking—and even ironic—that some commentators critical of the papalism and even ultramontanism that have

119

emerged since the nineteenth century have hung on every word of the present pope; one Catholic periodical in the United States even runs a laudatory feature, "Francis, the comic strip." I admire the simple gospel wisdom contained in much of the pope's daily preaching, for instance, but have reservations concerning the papal reach into the daily lives of believers and parishes: priests' daily homilies sometimes merely rehash what the pope said earlier that morning. It is not a good sign when priests, bishops, or cardinals (or laity) become echo chambers of the pope, whomever—and however insightful—he may be. Initiative in the church should not come always or even primarily from the "center." Bishops are, according to *Lumen gentium* (no. 27), "vicars and legates of Christ" in their own dioceses; they are not branch managers of an international corporation. The ongoing task is, as retired Cardinal Godfried Danneels of Belgium has said, to foster a "strong Peter" and a "strong episcopal college." The solution, he notes, "cannot be to dance on one foot"![26] It is encouraging in this regard that Pope Francis has encouraged the bishops—and, by extension, all of the faithful—to take the initiative in speaking openly and forthrightly.

CONCLUSION

The relationship between the local and universal church inevitably and inherently involves structural reforms. It can be no other way in a church that, in the words of *Lumen gentium* (no. 8), is "one complex reality comprising a human and a divine element." And, there can be no doubt that Pope Francis has already done much to advance necessary and often overdue reforms. Still, as he reminded the cardinals gathered in advance of the February 2015 consistory,

Reform is not an end in itself, but a means to bear a stronger Christian testimony; to favor a more effective evangelization; to promote a more fruitful ecumenical spirit; to encourage a more constructive dialogue with all. The reform, actively sought by most Cardinals in the context of the general Congregations before the Conclave, will still have to further refine the identity of the Roman Curia itself, in other words, that of assisting Peter's Successor in the exercise of his supreme pastoral office for the good and the service of the Universal Church and the Particular Churches. It is an exercise with which the unity of faith and the communion of the People of God are strengthened and the very mission of the Church in the world is advanced.[27]

These "structural" reforms are thus inextricably linked to, and driven by, the pope's repeated calls—especially to church leaders—for spiritual reform, for conversion. He does so "positively," as with his address in February 2014 to the Congregation for Bishops, outlining the characteristics of the ideal bishop.[28] And, he does so "negatively," as with his withering attack at Christmas 2014 on fifteen "diseases" that threaten workers in the Roman Curia (and in the church as a whole).[29] The "Pope of Mercy" does not hesitate to criticize and to scold!

Perhaps most appealing, though, is the manifest confidence with which he carries out his papal ministry. Once again, Yves Congar's comments on John XXIII are apposite: "[He] had confidence in human beings, had confidence in the Church, which he allowed to express itself freely. That was the secret of opening up that he achieved."[30] It is that mixture of evangelical boldness and simple humanity that makes Pope Francis an attractive witness. His mission—and the church's—is to foster harmony in the Holy Spirit, to enable brothers and sisters to "live together in unity" (Ps 133:1) so that the world may believe that the Father has sent the Son for its salvation. Everything that concerns the relationship of the local and universal churches is but a means to that "work of our redemption" (*Sacrosanctum concilium* 2) accomplished in Christ's self-giving on the cross and made present in the Eucharist celebrated by each local church in communion with the Church of Rome and its Bishop and with the whole church. In Christ alone do "all things hold together" (Col 1:17).

NOTES

1. Walter Kasper, "On the Church," *The Tablet* 255 (June 23, 2001): 927–30; Joseph Ratzinger, "The Local Church and the Universal Church: A Response to Walter Kasper," *America* 185 (November 19, 2001): 7–11; Walter Kasper, "From the President of the Pontifical Council for Promoting Christian Unity," *America* 185 (November 26, 2001): 28–29.

2. Yves Congar, *My Journal of the Council*, trans. Mary John Ronayne and Mary Cecily Boulding (Collegeville, MN: Michael Glazier/Liturgical Press, 2012), 304.

3. Jorge Bergoglio, "Bergoglio's Intervention: A Diagnosis of the Problems in the Church," March 27, 2013, http://en.radio vaticana.va/storico/2013/03/27/bergoglios_intervention_a_diag nosis_of_the_problems_in_the_church/en1-677269.

4. Ibid.

5. Pope Francis, "World Youth Day 2013: Meeting with CELAM Leaders," *Origins* 43 (August 22, 2013): 206–10, at 209.

6. Pope Francis, "Consistory Creates 20 New Cardinals," *Origins* 44 (February 26, 2015): 620–21, at 621.

7. Pope Francis also develops the theme of unity-in-diversity through the prism of the Holy Spirit. One example: "It is true that the Holy Spirit brings forth different charisms in the Church, which at first glance, may seem to create disorder. Under his guidance, however, they constitute an immense richness, because the Holy Spirit is the Spirit of unity, which is not the same thing as uniformity. Only the Holy Spirit is able to kindle diversity, multiplicity and, at the same time, bring about unity. When we try to create diversity, but are closed within our own particular and exclusive ways of seeing things, we create division. When we try to create unity through our own human designs, we end up with uniformity and homogenization. If we let ourselves be led by the Spirit, how-ever, richness, variety and diversity will never create conflict, because the Spirit spurs us to experience variety in the communion

of the Church." (Pope Francis, "Turkey Visit: Mass in Holy Spirit Cathedral," *Origins* 44 [December 11, 2014]: 469–70, at 469.)

8. Pope Francis, "World Youth Day 2013: Meeting with CELAM Leaders," 207.

9. Richard Gaillardetz, "The 'Francis Moment': A New Kairos for Catholic Ecclesiology," *CTSA Proceedings* 69 (2014): 63–80, at 67–72.

10. See Yves Congar's pointed comment, in his conciliar diary entry of March 12, 1963: "It would seem that the Romans want above all to cut, at its root, any attempt to establish, in whatever form, a permanent council around the pope. Because that would be the end of their reign and the destruction of what they have built up with such dogged patience over the past fifteen centuries." (Congar, *My Journal of the Council*, 280).

11. Pope Francis, "Homily at Mass with New Cardinals," *Origins* 44 (February 26, 2015): 617–20, at 619.

12. Cindy Wooden, "Feed My Sheep: Archbishops to Receive Palliums at Home with Their Flock," *Catholic News Service*, January 29, 2015, http://www.thecompassnews.org/2015/01/feed-sheep-archbishops-receive-palliums-home-flock/.

13. Elise Harris, "Pope Says Palliums Will Be Given to New Archbishops at Home—Not Rome," *Catholic News Agency*, January 29, 2015, http://www.catholicnewsagency.com/news/pope-says-palliums-will-be-given-to-new-archbishops-at-home-not-rome-38692.

14. J.-M.R. Tillard, *I Believe, Despite Everything: Reflections of an Ecumenist*, trans. William G. Rusch (Collegeville, MN: Unitas/Liturgical Press, 2003), 30.

15. *Evangelii gaudium*, for instance, mentions "discernment" eleven times.

16. See Pope Francis, *A Big Heart Open to God: A Conversation with Pope Francis, Interview by Antonio Spadaro* (New York: HarperOne/America, 2013), 33.

17. Ibid., 48–50.

18. See John W. O'Malley, *The First Jesuits* (Cambridge, MA: Harvard, 1993), 371.

19. See Jorge Mario Bergoglio/Pope Francis, *In Him Alone Is Our Hope: Spiritual Exercises Given to His Brother Bishops in the*

Manner of Saint Ignatius of Loyola, trans. Vincent Capuano and Andrew Matt (New York: Magnificat, 2013).

20. See John R. Quinn, *The Reform of the Papacy: The Costly Call to Christian Unity* (New York: Crossroad, 1999), 113. Also, Michael A. Fahey, "The Synod of America: Reflections of a Nonparticipant," *Theological Studies* 59 (1998): 486–504, at 503.

21. Pope Francis, "Greeting of Pope Francis to the Synod Fathers during the First General Congregation of the Third Extraordinary General Assembly of the Synod of Bishops," October 6, 2014, http://w2.vatican.va/content/francesco/en/speeches/2014/october/documents/papa-francesco_20141006_padri-sinodali.html.

22. See Russell Shaw, *Nothing to Hide: Secrecy, Communication, and Communion in the Catholic Church* (San Francisco: Ignatius, 2008).

23. J.-M.R. Tillard, *The Bishop of Rome*, trans. John de Satgé (Wilmington, DE: Michael Glazier, 1983), 1, 45, 47, 62, 193.

24. See Joseph A. Komonchak, "Modernity and the Construction of Roman Catholicism," *Cristianesimo nella storia* 18 (1997): 353–85, at 372–73; J.-M.R. Tillard, "Théologies et 'devotions' au pape depuis le Moyen Âge. De Jean XXIII à…Jean XXIII," *Cristianesimo nella storia* 22 (2001): 191–211.

25. Quoted in Paul Elie, "The Pope in the Attic: Benedict in the Time of Francis," *The Atlantic* 313 (April 2014): 46–54, at 48.

26. Godfried Danneels, "The Contemporary Person and the Church," *America* 185 (July 30, 2001): 6–9, at 7.

27. Pope Francis, "Greeting of the Holy Father to Cardinals Gathered for the Consistory," February 12, 2015, http://w2.vatican.va/content/francesco/en/speeches/2015/february/documents/papa-francesco_20150212_saluto-concistoro-cardinali.html.

28. Pope Francis, "Bishops Should Be Evangelists, Not CEOs," *Origins* 43 (March 20, 2014): 665–69.

29. Pope Francis, "Christmas Greetings to Curia Officials," *Origins* 44 (January 8, 2015): 505–10.

30. Congar, *My Journal of the Council*, 305.

CHAPTER 8

THE PASTORAL ORIENTATION OF DOCTRINE

Richard R. Gaillardetz

Pope Francis has quickly established himself as a defender of the proper place of doctrine in the church. On the surface, this is an odd claim. When we think of popes noted for their defense of doctrine, we may recall Pope Pius IX and his 1864 *Syllabus of Errors* or Pope Pius XII, the last pope to solemnly define a dogma (the bodily assumption of Mary). We might even consider Francis's immediate predecessor, Pope Benedict XVI, who is a respected dogmatic theologian who toiled for two decades as the Prefect for the Congregation for the Doctrine of the Faith before being elected Bishop of Rome. Pope Francis, however, is viewed by some as a threat to the church's doctrinal heritage, offering in evidence his openness to extending eucharistic Communion to the divorced and remarried.

In fact, Pope Francis has been careful to reaffirm controverted teachings on birth control, abortion, the indissolubility of marriage, and the prohibition of same-sex marriage.[1] In this chapter, we will examine the distinctive contribution that Pope Francis makes to our doctrinal tradition not by revising church doctrine, solemnly defining new dogma, or vigorously defending current doctrine, but rather by recontextualizing doctrine in service of the church's pastoral mission. Francis is advancing a central feature of the teaching of the Second Vatican Council; its commitment to what Christoph Theobald has coined "the pastorality of doctrine."[2]

POPE SAINT JOHN XXIII AND VATICAN II ON THE PASTORAL ORIENTATION OF DOCTRINE

In Pope Saint John XXIII's influential opening address at the council, *Gaudet mater ecclesia*, he offered an unambiguous affirmation of the church's fidelity to its doctrinal heritage. However, he also insisted that fidelity to the church's doctrinal heritage means more than the rote repetition of doctrinal formulas:

> The whole world expects a step forward toward a doctrinal penetration and a formation of consciousness in faithful and perfect conformity to the authentic doctrine, which, however, should be studied and expounded through the methods of research and through the literary forms of modern thought. The substance of the ancient doctrine of the deposit of faith is one thing, and the way in which it is presented is another.[3]

The pope exhibited an understanding of doctrine quite different from what was found in the neoscholastic manual tradition. That tradition had dominated Catholic theology and catechesis in the decades prior to the Council. It viewed divine revelation in static categories as a collection of free-floating doctrinal propositions the meaning of which was self-evident. The manual tradition offered what Juan Segundo calls a "digital" view of doctrine that is purged of its mystagogical and transformative character and rendered strictly regulative and informational.[4] According to Pope John, by contrast, doctrine is rooted in particular historical contexts and has to be studied "through the methods of research and through the literary forms of modern thought." Most doctrinal teachings emerged in the church not as theoretical proposals but as determinate responses to particular church crises or challenges. The appropriate pastoral application of a church doctrine requires that one knows something of the historical and pastoral context in which a teaching first emerged. In addition, as the pope insisted, the church must always be open to the possibility that a doctrine may need to be reformulated in ways that better express its deep meaning and that are more conducive to its proper communication in the modern age.

From this more sophisticated appeal to church doctrine, Pope John then offered a critical assessment of the way in which church teaching authority had been exercised in the past. An emphasis on the vigorous condemnation of error must be replaced, he insisted, by the "medicine of mercy" and by persuasively demonstrating the truth of church teaching. This requires a teaching magisterium that is fundamentally pastoral in character. The church must not be content with offering a mere repetition of doctrinal formulations; what is demanded is a penetration of church doctrine in view of the pressing questions of our age.

The council followed the pope's lead and consistently avoided treating the qualifiers *doctrinal* and *pastoral* as if they referred to different aspects of the church. The Council presented church doctrine as something to be authentically interpreted and faithfully applied within concrete historical, cultural, and pastoral contexts. John O'Brien observes that with the work of the Council, the "pastoral had regained its proper standing as something far more than the mere application of doctrine but as the very context from which doctrines emerge, the very condition of the possibility of doctrine, the touchstone for the validity of doctrine and the always prior and posterior praxis which doctrine at most, attempts to sum up, safeguard, and transmit."[5]

The Council bishops did not renounce the need for church doctrine but rather placed church teaching in the context of a much richer theology of revelation as God's self-communication, an invitation to divine friendship (*Dei verbum* 2). Although the fullness of divine revelation was communicated in the person of Jesus, the church does not possess a comprehensive and exhaustive grasp of that revelation. Rather, the Council taught that the church lives in history moving "toward the fullness of divine truth" (DV 8). The church does not so much possess revelation as it is possessed by it; the church is called to live into divine truth.

This rich theology of revelation inserts doctrine within the broader framework of God's sharing of God's self with humanity. This recontextualization of doctrine invites a form of doctrinal humility. Catherine Cornille observes that, prior to the Council, when humility was related to doctrine, "it has more often been regarded as an attitude to be adopted *toward* rather than *about* the truth of Christian doctrines."[6] Individual Christians were reminded of the limits of human reason and exhorted to a humble posture of docile obedience in the face of the authority of doctrine. The Second Vatican Council invites us to a new form of "doctrinal humility." This doctrinal humility is evident in the Council's insistence that Revelation not be treated as a divine answer book providing definitive solutions to all the questions of our time:

> The Church guards the heritage of God's word and draws from it moral and religious principles without always having at hand the solution to particular problems. As such she desires to add the light of revealed truth to mankind's store of experience, so that the path which humanity has taken in recent times will not be a dark one. (GS 33)

This more measured appraisal of the place of church doctrine is also evident in the Council's teaching on the "hierarchy of truths": "When comparing doctrines with one another, they should remember that in Catholic doctrine there exists a "hierarchy" of truths, since they vary in their relation to the fundamental Christian faith" (UR 11).[7] In this brief passage, the Council introduced a crucial distinction between the *content* of divine revelation, understood as God's self-communication in Christ by the power of the Spirit, and those church doctrines that, in varying degrees, *mediate* that content. In this context, doctrinal humility means recognizing that, although church doctrine may mediate divine revelation, it never exhausts it.

Finally, Theobald reminds us that the Council affirmed the intrinsically pastoral orientation of doctrine by attending to the recipients of the church's teaching.[8] The gospel is proclaimed to ordinary people within particular historical, cultural, and social contexts: "For, from the beginning of her [the church's] history she has learned to express the message of Christ with the help of the ideas and terminology of various philosophers, and has tried to clarify it with their wisdom, too" (GS 44). This theme would reappear in the Decree on the Church's Missionary Activity (*Ad gentes*) where the Council imagines the Word of God as a "seed" that is always planted in the distinctive soil of a local culture (AG 22). Doctrine can never be fully grasped apart from that cultural context.

We might say, by way of summary, that the Second Vatican Council understood church doctrine as formal teaching that must be authentically interpreted and applied (1) in the light of the historical context in which the doctrine was first articulated; (2) within a trinitarian theology of revelation and the fundamental Christian message or kerygma that doctrine mediates but does not exhaust; and (3) in view of the recipients of church teaching who receive and make church doctrine their own in particular cultural contexts.

POPE FRANCIS ON THE PASTORAL ORIENTATION OF DOCTRINE

Pope Francis's four most recent predecessors were all participants at the Council. Of the four, Blessed Pope Paul VI, Pope Saint John Paul II, and Pope Benedict XVI each carried forward distinct elements of conciliar teaching. At the same time, significant conciliar themes were either neglected entirely or given only a cursory nod. Although Pope Francis was not ordained a priest until four years after the Council's close, his biographer, Austen Ivereigh, contends, "The Council would be Bergoglio's greatest teacher, and the single greatest source, later, of his pontificate."[9] This pope has boldly returned to the foreground a broad range of neglected conciliar teachings and foremost among them is the Council's pastoral orientation toward doctrine. Francis's approach to church doctrine has two features: first, he relates doctrine to something more fundamental, the basic Christian message; second, he insists that doctrine must always be interpreted with attention to pastoral context.

DOCTRINE AND THE HIERARCHY OF TRUTHS

In his address at the plenary session of the Congregation for the Doctrine of the Faith in January 2014, Pope Francis distilled his understanding of doctrine into one sentence: "In reality, doctrine has the sole purpose of serving the life of the People of God and it seeks to assure our faith of a sure foundation."[10] Doctrine plays a necessary role in the life of the church, but it should not be used as an excuse for suppressing disagreement and doubt. Few if any modern popes have spoken so honestly about the positive place of doubt and the dangers of false certitude:

> If one has the answers to all the questions—that is the proof that God is not with him. It means that he is a false prophet using religion for himself. The great leaders of the people of God, like Moses, have always left room for doubt.[11]

Neither should doctrine and church discipline be used as a way of silencing those who propose new pastoral avenues. When speaking to the leadership of CELAM, Francis warned of a form of ecclesial Pelagianism:

> This basically appears as a form of restorationism. In dealing with the Church's problems, a purely disciplinary

solution is sought, through the restoration of outdated manners and forms which, even on the cultural level, are no longer meaningful. In Latin America it is usually to be found in small groups, in some new religious congregations, in tendencies to doctrinal or disciplinary "safety." Basically it is static, although it is capable of inversion, in a process of regression. It seeks to "recover" the lost past.[12]

In an open letter to the founder of the Italian newspaper *La Repubblica*, Eugenio Scalfari, the pope admitted a reluctance to speak of "absolute truth," not because he was a "relativist" but because, for Christians, truth is mediated through a relationship with a person, Christ. As such, truth is always encountered in history.[13] Pope Francis insists that doctrine be comprehended in relation to this more basic Christian message. Consider his retrieval of one of the most neglected themes of the council, the "hierarchy of truths."

In the five decades following Vatican II, there has been little recourse to the hierarchy of truths in magisterial documents. In an important study of the topic, Catherine Clifford uncovers but a single papal reference to the hierarchy of truths prior to Pope Francis.[14] Our current pope, however, has eagerly taken up the theme:

All revealed truths derive from the same divine source and are to be believed with the same faith, yet some of them are more important for giving direct expression to the heart of the Gospel. In this basic core, what shines forth is the beauty of the saving love of God made manifest in Jesus Christ who died and rose from the dead. In this sense, the Second Vatican Council explained, "in Catholic doctrine there exists an order or a 'hierarchy' of truths, since they vary in their relation to the foundation of the Christian faith." This holds true as much for the dogmas of faith as for the whole corpus of the Church's teaching, including her moral teaching. (*EG* 36)

Francis rightly acknowledges that the Council's teaching on the hierarchy of truths is more than a matter of ranking doctrines; the Council wished to relate doctrine to something more basic, the Christian kerygma. For Francis, too, doctrine is always at the service of the fundamental Christian message. This is because the language of doctrine is a kind of second-order language that expresses in precise propositional terms the central convictions of the Christian faith. This more formal, propositional language inevitably puts doctrine at several degrees of abstraction from the gospel as it is experienced concretely in the life of discipleship. Pope Francis writes,

> Pastoral ministry in a missionary style is not obsessed with the disjointed transmission of a multitude of doctrines to be insistently imposed. When we adopt a pastoral goal and a missionary style which would actually reach everyone without exception or exclusion, the message has to concentrate on the essentials, on what is most beautiful, most grand, most appealing and at the same time most necessary. The message is simplified, while losing none of its depth and truth, and thus becomes all the more forceful and convincing. (EG 35)

Francis is not afraid to affirm the necessary place of doctrine in the church, but he consistently orients that doctrine toward the core Christian kerygma and situates it within the pastoral life of the church.

THE PASTORAL CONTEXTUALIZATION OF DOCTRINE

Pope Francis's commitment to the pastoral orientation of doctrine is evident in his treatment of three controversial issues:

the pastoral care of the divorced and remarried, the interpretation of *Humanae vitae*, and the pastoral care of homosexuals.

The Extraordinary Synod on the Family that was convened in the fall of 2014 and the Ordinary Synod on the Family in the fall of 2015 are addressing a broad range of pastoral issues. Among them is a matter of longstanding concern for Pope Francis, namely, pastoral care for the divorced and remarried, those who are excluded from the sacrament of the Eucharist. Pope Francis has no wish to revise the church's teaching on the indissolubility of marriage. His intention, rather, is to root the church's teaching more firmly within the field of Christian mercy. Can we recognize that there are at least some divorced and remarried couples who find themselves in a situation in which renouncing their second marriage would compound the harm caused by the failure of the first marriage and require breaking current familial commitments? In such a pastoral situation, is it not possible, he is asking, to find signs of grace and hope and to recognize the value of the Eucharist for such couples as "a medicine of mercy" (EG 47)? Pope Francis exemplifies a determination to negotiate the tension between the normative claims of church doctrine and pastoral reality, that is, the concrete situations of Christians who find themselves in particular circumstances that impose their own specific demands and obligations. He refuses to see doctrine and pastoral practice as mutually exclusive options; rather, he insists that it is possible to preserve the very tension that many wish to resolve prematurely. The temptation to resolve artificially this tension comes in several forms. As noted earlier, in his address at the conclusion of the Extraordinary Synod on the Family in October of 2014, the pope warned against

> a temptation to hostile inflexibility, that is, wanting to close oneself within the written word, (the letter) and not allowing oneself to be surprised by God, by the God of surprises, (the spirit); within the law, within the certitude of what we know and not of what we still

need to learn and to achieve. From the time of Christ, it is the temptation of the zealous, of the scrupulous, of the solicitous and of the so-called—today—"traditionalists" and also of the intellectuals.[15]

Yet he also warned of "the temptation to neglect the '*depositum fidei*' [the deposit of faith], not thinking of themselves as guardians, but as owners or masters [of it]." As the church prepares for the Ordinary Synod on the Family in the fall of 2015, Francis calls the church to have the courage to undergo honest discernment and humble listening.

Let us consider a second example of Francis's pastoral appropriation of church teaching. In one of his many interviews, the pope was asked directly about Pope Paul VI's teaching in *Humanae vitae* on artificial birth regulation:

> It all depends on how the text of "*Humanae Vitae*" is interpreted. Paul VI himself, towards the end, recommended to confessors much mercy and attention to concrete situations. But his genius was prophetic, as he had the courage to go against the majority, to defend moral discipline, to apply a cultural brake, to oppose present and future neo-Malthusianism. The object is not to change the doctrine, but it is a matter of going into the issue in depth and to ensure that the pastoral ministry takes into account the situations of each person and what that person can do. This will also be discussed on the path to the Synod.[16]

Later, during his visit to the Philippines, he again reaffirmed the teaching of Paul VI, noting again, that Pope Paul was courageous to challenge the cultural preoccupation with population control. At the same time, Francis counseled confessors to "be very generous" in dealing with individual couples' pastoral situations.[17] On the plane home from that trip, he insisted that fidelity to church teaching on birth control must be interpreted within the context of the Second Vatican Council's call for "responsible parenthood," and he warned that fidelity to church teaching doesn't mean that married couples should "breed like rabbits."

In these various statements and interviews, there are echoes of John XXIII's call for a deeper penetration of church doctrine and its more pastoral realization. Note that while Pope Francis insists on fidelity to *Humanae vitae*, there is no mention of the specific injunction that every conjugal act must be open to conception. It is unclear what his attitude is regarding this moral injunction, but his interests do not seem to align well with the "theology of the body" devotees who focus on a narrow moral analysis of the "conjugal act."[18] Instead, Francis redirects our attention to the larger prophetic thrust of the encyclical. He offers the wise acknowledgment, too often lacking among critics of *Humanae vitae*, that Paul VI was prescient regarding the dangerous allure of a contraceptive mentality that technologizes and even commodifies human reproduction in contemporary Western culture. The reference to "neo-Malthusianism" recalls the 1968 CELAM meeting at Medellín at which the Latin American bishops not only supported a liberationist interpretation of the Council but also voiced their support for *Humanae vitae*. In the 1968 Latin American context, the promotion of artificial birth control was viewed as the attempt of a rich first world elite to control an expanding poor population.

Francis insists that the central values embedded in the doctrine must be applied in ways that "[take] into account the situations of each person and what that person can do." This is not a pastoral compromise regarding church teaching, but an authentic interpretation of the doctrine as it relates to real human persons and the concrete narrative framework within which they must make specific moral decisions. Francis is modeling a methodology of moral discernment that broadens our moral reflection beyond a narrow analysis of an act to consider the human person as a whole. It is a process of moral reflection that must always consider the larger social context of any contemplated moral action.

Finally, we can consider the pope's controversial remarks on homosexuality encapsulated in his oft-quoted and just as frequently misunderstood statement, "Who am I to judge?" The statement was offered in response to a journalist mentioning the case of a Vatican priest who was known to be gay. At no point has Pope Francis called for a recognition of same-sex marriages either civilly or sacramentally. Yet given that Pope Francis handpicked the drafting committee for the *relatio post disceptationem* at the Extraordinary Synod on the Family, it is not difficult to imagine that he would support the following statement found in that remarkable report:

> Homosexuals have gifts and qualities to offer to the Christian community: are we capable of welcoming these people, guaranteeing to them a fraternal space in our communities? Often they wish to encounter a Church that offers them a welcoming home. Are our communities capable of providing that, accepting and valuing their sexual orientation, without compromising Catholic doctrine on the family and matrimony?... Without denying the moral problems connected to homosexual unions it has to be noted that there are cases in which mutual aid to the point of sacrifice constitutes a precious support in the life of the partners.[19]

How shall we characterize the position of the pope on this complicated issue? John Langan appeals to something very much like the pastoral orientation of doctrine, claiming that Pope Francis was not concerned with either a simple reaffirmation or a reversal of the church's official teaching on homosexuality, but rather with a thorough reconsideration of the church's "stance." For Langan, "stance" is distinct from a specific doctrinal formulation. To consider the church's "stance" on an issue calls for "critical reflection on the tradition to clarify what strengths are to be preserved and what continuities are to be affirmed even while searching for the sources of limitations in the teaching and acknowledging the development of new questions and problems."[20] A change in stance may or may not bring about a change in church doctrine. What it does allow for is a consideration of hitherto neglected factors and insights.

For many, Langan's proposal that we focus on a change in stance will not go far enough. They will continue to press the question: Will or will not this pope reverse this or that controversial church teaching? However, the "will he or won't he" question misconstrues how doctrine develops. It is a common misconception that doctrinal change and development occur primarily by ecclesiastical fiat. In fact, history shows that doctrine changes when pastoral contexts shift and new insights emerge such that particular doctrinal formulations no longer mediate the saving message of God's transforming love. The gradual shift in the church's condemnation of usury offers us a classic example of what I have in mind here. That teaching was not reversed in a single papal decree. Rather, there was a gradual and halting pastoral discernment that the teaching, in its classical formulation, no longer served the central values it was intended to protect, namely the welfare of the poor.[21] Eamon Duffy explains the more circumscribed role of papal teaching in this process: "'Definitive' papal utterances are not oracles providing new information, but adjudications at the end of a wider and longer process of doctrinal reflection, consultation, and debate, often extending over centuries."[22] Magisterial teaching should come at the end of our tradition's lively engagement with a particular question, not as a way of preempting its consideration.

Certainly, church leaders are to be faithful to our doctrinal heritage. They serve that heritage best, not by wielding the doctrine of the church as a club, but by heeding Pope Francis's injunction to abandon a place of safety and certitude, moving from the center to the periphery. As they meet the people "in the streets," listening to their concerns and attending to their wounds, they will know, through a pastoral "connaturality," how the church's doctrine can best be employed to announce God's solidarity with the poor and suffering of this world and the profligate mercy of God. This is the primary purpose of church doctrine, and in reminding us of this, Francis stands as its authentic guardian.

NOTES

1. Some of this material is drawn from Richard R. Gaillardetz, "The 'Francis Moment': A New *Kairos* for Catholic Ecclesiology," *CTSA Proceedings* 69 (2014): 63–80.

2. Christoph Theobald, "The Theological Options of Vatican II: Seeking an 'Internal' Principle of Interpretation," in *Vatican II: A Forgotten Future, Concilium* 2005, no.4 (2005): 87–107.

3. Pope John's opening address may be accessed online at http://conciliaria.com/2012/10/mother-church-rejoices-opening-address-of-john-xxiii-at-the-council/#more-2134.

4. For an articulation and critique of this digital approach to doctrine, see Juan Luis Segundo, *The Liberation of Dogma: Faith, Revelation and Dogmatic Teaching Authority*, trans. Philip Berryman (Maryknoll, NY: Orbis, 1992), 108.

5. John O'Brien, "Ecclesiology as Narrative," *Ecclesiology* 4, no. 2 (2008): 150.

6. Catherine Cornille, *The Im-possibility of Interreligious Dialogue* (New York: Crossroad, 2008), 27–28.

7. Translations of conciliar documents are taken from Austin Flannery, *Vatican Council II: Constitutions, Decrees, Declarations*, rev. ed. (Collegeville, MN: Liturgical Press, 1996).

8. Christoph Theobald, "The Principle of Pastorality at Vatican II: Challenges of a Prospective Interpretation of the Council," in *The Legacy of Vatican II*, ed. Massimo Faggioli and Andrew Vicini (New York: Paulist Press, 2015), 26–37, at 28.

9. Austen Ivereigh, *The Great Reformer: Francis and the Making of a Radical Pope* (New York: Henry Holt, 2014), 57.

10. Pope Francis, "Address to the Congregation for the Doctrine of the Faith," January 31, 2014, http://www.zenit.org/en/articles/pope-francis-address-to-congregation-for-the-doctrine-of-the-faith.

11. Pope Francis, "A Big Heart Open to God," *America* (September 30, 2013), http://americamagazine.org/pope-interview.

12. This address can be accessed online at http://www.vati can.va/holy_father/francesco/speeches/2013/july/documents/pa pa-francesco_20130728_gmg-celam-rio_en.html.

13. Pope Francis, "Letter to a Non-Believer," http://w2.vati can.va/content/francesco/en/letters/2013/documents/papa-francesco_20130911_eugenio-scalfari.html.

14. It is found in Pope John Paul II's encyclical on ecu-menism, *Ut unum sint* 37, where it appears, however, without any developed explication or application. This document can be accessed at http://www.vatican.va/holy_father/john_paul_ii/ encyclicals/documents/hf_jp-ii_enc_25051995_ut-unum-sint _en.html. See Catherine Clifford, "L'herméneutique d'un principe herméneutique: La hiérarchie des vérités," in *L'Autorité et les autorités: L'herméneutique théologique de Vatican II*, ed. Gilles Routhier and Guy Jobin (Paris: Cerf, 2010), 69–91, at 70.

15. This papal address is available online at https://w2.vati can.va/content/francesco/en/speeches/2014/october/documents /papa-francesco_20141018_conclusione-sinodo-dei-vescovi.html.

16. The transcript of the interview can be accessed online at http://www.catholicnewsagency.com/news/transcript-pope-fran cis-march-5-interview-with-corriere-della-sera/.

17. John L. Allen Jr., "Pope Francis Criticizes Gay Marriage, Backs Ban on Contraception," in *Crux*, http://www.cruxnow.com/ church/2015/01/16/pope-francis-criticizes-gay-marriage-backs-contraception-ban/.

18. For a perceptive reflection on the reductive dangers attendant to focusing on sex as a "conjugal act," see Maureen Mullarkey, "Killing Sex to Save It," *First Things*, December 15, 2014, https://www.firstthings.com/tag/sexuality/page_2.

19. "*Relatio post disceptationem* for 2014 Synod of Bishops on the family," *NCR Online* (October 15, 2014): nos. 50–51, http://ncronline.org/news/vatican/relatio-post-disceptationem-2014-synod-bishops-family.

20. John P. Langan, "See the Person," *America* (March 10, 2014): 14.

21. See John Noonan's still classic treatment of this in *The Scholastic Analysis of Usury* (Cambridge, MA: Harvard University Press, 1957); and *The Church that Can and Cannot Change* (Notre Dame, IN: Univ. of Notre Dame Press, 2005).

22. Eamon Duffy, "Who is the Pope?" *New York Times Review of Books* (February 19, 2015), http://www.nybooks.com/articles /archives/2015/feb/19/who-is-pope-francis/.

CHAPTER 9

MINISTRY AS MERCIFUL ACCOMPANIMENT

Richard Lennan

Every pope bears a twofold responsibility within the church. In addition to fostering the inner unity of the Christian community, the pope nurtures in all the baptized a commitment to discipleship in the daily living of the gospel. Those two aspects of the pope's office are inseparable, united by their common grounding in the trinitarian God: God's Holy Spirit is the agent of the church's unity, just as the love of Christ leads the church to engage the world with the hope of the gospel. While the pope must be attentive to both of these responsibilities, the circumstances of history are likely to result in one or other of the two being at the forefront of the pope's attention at any particular time.

Pope Francis's priority is the formation of disciples willing to respond generously to the suffering of today's world, which calls urgently to the church. A constant theme of Pope Francis's preaching and teaching is that the gospel summons members of the church to give flesh to God's merciful care for the world. Pervading *Evangelii gaudium* is the pope's conviction that the "Gospel joy which enlivens the community of disciples is a missionary joy" (EG 21), directing us outward. In the present moment of "epochal change" (no. 52), when "the majority of our contemporaries are barely living from day to day," marginalized from the benefits that "the enormous qualitative, quantitative, rapid and cumulative advances" in science and technology have conferred on a small proportion of the world's population (no. 52), the church is to be a "field hospital" for the world's wounded.[1]

As this chapter will illustrate, Pope Francis's stress on the mission of the church also colors his presentation of the church's ministry.[2] In order to bring into relief the characteristics of the latter, it will be helpful to review the recent history of Catholic practice and thought in relation to ministry.

"MINISTRY" IN CATHOLIC PRACTICE AND THEOLOGY

Ministry looms large in the modern Catholic lexicon, but the term was not always so prominent. Prior to the Second Vatican Council, when responsibility for the significant aspects of the church's life resided all but exclusively in ordained priests, the priest's identity as *alter Christus* ("another Christ") could overshadow the practice of ministry. The theologies of sacramental grace that prevailed among Catholics reinforced that emphasis by portraying priests as superior to the church's other members— "ordination gives priests a grace which is at once a capacity for and a call to sanctity higher than that of those who have simply been baptized."[3]

Vatican II brought "ministry" out of the shadows by underscoring that ordination was for the sake of service, rather than "power and honors" (*Optatum totius* 9). Although the Council applied "ministry" largely to the ordained, it recognized that "the faithful who by Baptism are incorporated into Christ, are placed in the People of God, and in their own way share in the priestly, prophetic and kingly office of Christ, and to the best of their ability carry on the mission of the whole Christian people in the Church and in the world" (*Lumen gentium* 31).[4] The latter description was pivotal in opening the way for lay members of the church to become ministers.

Over the last fifty years, the landscape of ministry has changed dramatically from what applied at the conclusion of Vatican II. "Shortage of priests" can function as a summary of one catalyst of change. In recent decades, local churches throughout the world have witnessed a significant downturn in the number of seminarians and those entering religious life, as well as large-scale resignations from the priesthood. Those trends have produced a widening gap between the number of Catholics and the supply of priests available to serve them.[5] That gap persists, even as many dioceses increase their reliance on elderly priests or adopt strategies such as the "clustering" of parishes, an innovation that revises radically the long-dominant paradigm under which a priest served exclusively in one, free-standing parish.

The other principal agent of change is the burgeoning of "lay ecclesial ministry." Although the emergence of lay ecclesial ministry, which is perhaps more prominent in the United States than elsewhere in the world, coincided with the altered situation of priests, it is far from being a product of it. Rather, as the expansive body of literature on the topic makes plain, lay ecclesial ministry, in accord with the Second Vatican Council's teaching cited previously, is a specific response that some lay members of the church make to the call of the Holy Spirit.[6] That call, which is expressed originally in baptism, is heard through the needs of others, amplified by the invitation of the ecclesial community to specific forms of service, and often endorsed officially by local ordinaries, as well as local communities. As the church's need for ministry has expanded in the last fifty years, increasing numbers of lay Catholics have accepted responsibility for meeting those needs.

Taken together, the present experiences of both the ordained and of lay ecclesial ministers indicate that the church is now in uncharted waters. Indeed, the evolution of ministry over the last fifty years has outstripped both the theological thinking that dominated less fluid eras in the history of ministry and the categories that the church's official teaching has traditionally applied to ministry.[7] The current dynamics of ministry have also generated various forms of anxiety in the church. For lay ecclesial ministers, the longing is often for better definition and recognition.[8] For ordained priests, the anxiety is encapsulated in the fabled "identity crisis" among priests; reference to "a crisis in the Catholic priesthood" became so familiar after Vatican II that, as early as 1969, one commentator declared the phrase to be already "hackneyed."[9] In the midst of this flux, the church's teaching authority has insisted on a sharp distinction between lay and ordained ministers.[10] The desire of many parties for a comprehensive delineation of the different forms of ministry in the church has produced, as Kathleen Cahalan remarks perceptively, a concentration on "the theology of the minister," a concentration that can eclipse "the theology of the doing of ministry."[11]

Pope Francis, however, reverses that ordering: he directs his energy towards enhancing the practice of ministry in the church, rather than dwelling on questions of ministerial identity. Significantly, he refers to the challenges, temptations, and opportunities confronting "pastoral workers" (EG 76–109), a category that includes the ordained, professed religious, and laypeople; he does not concern himself with reinforcing distinctions between them. Although the pope does address issues specific to the ordained priesthood, as we will observe, his overarching concern is with the characteristics of authentic ministry in the church, rather than the canonical status of the minister.

THE MINISTRY OF THE OPEN DOOR

The emphasis on mercy that has become a hallmark of Pope Francis's papacy, furthering his work among the poor as a bishop in Argentina, is integral to his presentation of the church's ministry. Francis identifies ministers, whether ordained or lay, as those "who accompany their brothers and sisters in faith or on a journey of openness to God" (EG 44). Echoing the stress on gradualism—

another of his hallmarks, Francis contends that accompaniment is to be done "with mercy and patience," attentive to "the eventual stages of growth as these progressively occur" (no. 44). Pope Francis regards ministers as "ostiaries" (doorkeepers), whose principal task is to be agents of God's mercy for those in need of it. Consequently, ministers must ensure that they do not set limits to God's mercy: "Who am I to change the ministry of the ostiary in a Church that, instead of opening, closes doors? Who am I to say 'here and no further'? Who am I to cage the Holy Spirit?"[12]

Pope Francis invokes often the sacrament of God's forgiveness as an instance in which ordained priests can be agents of God's mercy, mercy that is the antithesis of turning the confessional into a "torture chamber" (EG 44). More generally, the pope stresses that ministers of the sacraments are not to act "as arbiters of grace rather than its facilitators;" they are not to obscure the mission of the church to be "the house of the Father, where there is a place for everyone, with all their problems" (no. 47).

Since "pastoral workers" have a unique role in the church's mission, Pope Francis portrays them as vulnerable to unique temptations. Primary among those temptations is "an inordinate concern for their personal freedom and relaxation, which leads them to see their work as a mere appendage to their life" (no. 78). Self-absorbed pastoral workers "resist giving themselves over completely to mission and thus end up in a state of paralysis and acedia" (no. 81). The pope paints a bleak picture of a church whose ministers can lose enthusiasm, succumb to "a tomb psychology," and display "a faint melancholy, lacking in hope" (no. 81). Still worse, ministers can become "querulous and disillusioned pessimists, 'sourpusses'" (no. 85), rather than ambassadors of joy. The alternative to the manifold forms of decay that can poison ministry is "breathing in the pure air of the Holy Spirit who frees us from self-centeredness cloaked in an outward religiosity bereft of God" (no. 97).

As Pope Francis outlines it, the likelihood that ministers will accompany others in life-giving ways depends significantly on the conversion of ministers away from self-absorption. Ministers who are thus converted act with reverence for others, a reverence that overcomes the isolation characteristic of contemporary life. Since God's offer of life in Christ is the opposite of all that is destructive, the pope is adamant that "ordained ministers and other pastoral workers are to make present the fragrance of Christ's closeness and his personal gaze" (no. 169). Pastoral workers fulfill that lofty vocation when they accompany people in a way that "heals, liberates, and encourages growth in the Christian life" (no. 169). Since growth in freedom takes time, accompaniment requires ministers willing to act with "prudence, understanding, patience and docility to the Spirit" (no. 171).

Such ministry is not a matter of technical efficiency. Rather, its defining characteristic is "respectful and compassionate listening," which Pope Francis presents as able to generate in its receivers "the desire to respond fully to God's love" (no. 171). Those who accompany, therefore, must be people who learn from their own experience "of being accompanied and assisted, and of openness to those who accompany us" (no. 172). Ministers who recognize the contours of their own growth in openness to Christ will understand that their role is not to judge others nor impose on them a timetable that demands their response.

Pope Francis reminds ministers that if they are to avoid "every kind of intrusive accompaniment or isolated self-realization" (no. 173), they must locate their activity in the context of the church's mission of evangelization. The import of that reminder is to reinforce the fact that evangelizers, like the church as a whole, must themselves "be evangelized," especially through God's word and the Eucharist (no. 174), but also through the poor, who "have much to teach us" (no. 198). Being shaped by the gospel is itself inseparable from sharing the life of those to whom the gospel is being offered: those who would evangelize, therefore, must "take on the 'smell of the sheep'" (no. 24). This link between ministry and the conversion of the minister—a link that Pope Francis highlights often—is also a consistent theme in his reflections on the ordained priesthood.

"PRIESTS ARE LIKE PLANES..."

Like every Bishop of Rome, Pope Francis refers frequently to the ministry of priests. What is perhaps less conventional about the present pope is the passionate spirit with which he appeals for greater authenticity in the lives of priests. In fact, Pope Francis's passion can generate the perception that he is inclined to "bash" priests, as he acknowledges.[13] However, the language that the pope employs when addressing priests does not proceed from a desire to humiliate them. Rather, the message to priests is a specific instance of his message to the church at large, a message that stresses the urgent need to be more attentive to "the voice of the Spirit speaking to the whole Church of our time, which is the time of mercy."[14]

At the heart of Pope Francis's references to the priesthood is the promotion of mercy: "For the love of Jesus Christ: never tire of being merciful! Please!"[15] The pope does not dwell on "the so-called crisis of priestly identity," but is tireless in encouraging priests to a renewed zeal for their ministry.[16] As Francis presents that ministry, it is intimately connected to the identity of the church mentioned previously: the church as "field hospital." Viewed in this light, the priest "is a man of mercy and compassion, close to his people and a servant to all....Whoever is wounded in life, in whatever way, can find in him attention and a sympathetic ear."[17]

While Pope Francis thus promotes a clear vision of priestly ministry, he is also alert to obvious deficits in the contemporary practice of the priesthood. One way in which he highlights both the possibilities and failings of the priesthood is his wordplay distinguishing between what it means for a priest to be "anointed" and to be "unctuous." In his homily at the Mass of the Chrism in both 2013 and 2014, for example, Pope Francis describes the priest as "the anointed one," an image that is prominent in Psalm 133 and applies paradigmatically to Christ himself. The pope stresses that as life flowed through Christ to others, so priests must "go out and give ourselves and the Gospel to others, giving what little ointment we have to those who have nothing, nothing at all."[18] He reminds priests that "the ointment is not intended just to make us fragrant, much less to be kept in a jar, for then it would become rancid…and the heart bitter."[19] Authentic priestly anointing produces "joy," rather than being something that "'greases' us, making us unctuous, sumptuous and presumptuous."[20] Here, the language illustrates starkly the difference between a genuine priesthood and one that is self-serving.

"Unctuous" priests, those "who place importance and power in artificial things, in vanities, those who have an affected attitude and way of speaking" and seem "like a butterfly because [they are] always fluttering about vanities," are regularly critiqued by Pope Francis.[21] In encouraging people to pray for priests and religious, therefore, he promotes prayer that asks God to "defend [priests] from the idolatry of vanity, from the idolatry of pride, from the idolatry of power, from the idolatry of money."[22]

Among the defects to which priests can succumb, "an excessive clericalism" is especially pernicious: by excluding lay members of the church from "decision-making" (EG 102), clericalism affects adversely the church's mission. Since it is women in the church who suffer most from the corrosive effects of clericalism, Pope Francis's condemnation of that vice leads him to acknowledge the "great challenge" that the church faces in relation to "the possible role of women in decision-making in different areas of the Church's life" (no. 103).

Pope Francis reaffirms his predecessors' teaching that the possibility of ordaining women to the priesthood "is not a question open to discussion" (no. 103). Nonetheless, he recognizes—albeit without articulating a strategy to achieve what he desires— the need for the presence and contribution of women "where important decisions are made, both in the Church and in social structures" (no. 103). In order to counter the exclusion of women from involvement in making decisions, the pope warns of the damage that results "if sacramental power is too closely identified with power in general" (no. 103). Ordination, then, does not license priests to exclude women from participating actively in the church.

As insidious as is clericalism, the horrific damage done to children who have been the victims of sexual abuse perpetrated by priests is the most tragic expression of the failure of priests to live what they profess. In condemning that abuse, Pope Francis portrays it as the most heinous form of idolatry: "It is something more than despicable actions. It is like a sacrilegious cult, because these boys and girls had been entrusted to the priestly charism in order to be brought to God. And those people sacrificed them to the idol of their own concupiscence. They profane the very image of God in whose likeness we were created."[23]

As an antidote for the many forms of "idolatry" to which priests are vulnerable, as a way to break the nexus between priests and "planes," which priests resemble in that "they only make the news when they crash, even though so many of them are in the air," Pope Francis proposes a two-fold strategy.[24] One aspect of that strategy is the need for greater discernment about the vocation of candidates for ordination. That discernment is especially urgent when the pressure to increase "numbers" tempts bishops to accept candidates indiscriminately: "Please, one must carefully study the evolution of a vocation! See whether it comes from the Lord, whether the man is healthy....Today we have so many problems, and in many dioceses, because some bishops made the mistake of taking those who at times have been expelled from other seminaries or religious houses because they need priests. Please! We must consider the good of the People of God."[25]

The formation of seminarians and those already ordained is the second area that Pope Francis highlights as contributing to an authentic priesthood. Here, he stresses that discipleship, a call that "draws one to Christ and conforms one ever more to him," makes a claim on the whole of one's life, rather than being mastered before ordination.[26] For this reason, the pope urges priests to remember that they are "the poorest of men unless Jesus enriches us by his poverty, the most useless of servants unless Jesus calls us his friends, the most ignorant of men unless Jesus patiently teaches him as he did Peter, the frailest of Christians unless the Good Shepherd strengthens him in the midst of the flock."[27]

Without a thoroughgoing relationship with Christ, priests are likely to mirror the various failings that Pope Francis associates particularly with the Roman Curia. Those failings include: the "Martha complex," which inclines clerics to regard themselves as being indispensable; "spiritual Alzheimer's disease," by which clerics who have lost sight of their encounter with God are "completely caught up in the present moment, in their passions, whims and obsessions; in those who build walls around themselves, and thus become more and more the slaves of idols carved by their own hands;" and the self-explanatory "disease of the lugubrious face."[28]

One aspect of priestly ministry to which Pope Francis devotes a great deal of attention in *Evangelii gaudium* is the homily. In part, that attention is the product of his conviction that the homily "surpasses all forms of catechesis as the supreme moment in the dialogue between God and his people" (EG 137). The pope is aware that such an ideal is not easy to realize, especially because the homily is the source of "so many concerns," indeed of "suffering," for the people in the pews and for priests (no. 135). As Pope Francis presents it, the key to an effective homily is a preacher who knows "the heart of his community, in order to realize where its desire for God is alive and ardent, as well as where that dialogue, once loving, has been thwarted and is now barren" (no. 137).

Viewed as a dimension of pastoral ministry, a good homily, while not "a form of entertainment like those presented by the media" (no. 138), is "a kind of music which inspires encouragement, strength and enthusiasm" (no. 139). Indeed, Pope Francis presents the homily as being akin to a mother addressing her children, who are receptive because they "know that they are loved" (no. 139). Whether all congregants and preachers would resonate with the "motherly" image of the homily is certainly an open question, but the pope's choice of words accords with his stress on the merciful love of God that all aspects of ministry are to reveal. It may be, however, that the pope's enthusiasm for merciful ministry leads him to overstate his case when he claims that the human qualities of the preacher, those evident in "the warmth of his voice, the unpretentiousness of his manner of speaking, the joy of his gestures," can bear fruit even when the homily "may be somewhat tedious" (no. 140).

Since preaching that involves "heart-to-heart communication" can have a "quasi-sacramental character," it differs markedly from a lecture on exegesis and from content that is "moralistic or doctrinaire" (no. 142). Integral to the possibility that a homily might express God's merciful love is the need for good preparation. So convinced is Pope Francis of the value of such preparation, he identifies it as a principal aspect of the priest's ministry "even if less time has to be given to other important activities" (no. 145). Preparation is far more than working on the mechanics of preaching; in fact, its core component is "serene concentration" on the biblical text (no. 146). Preachers, therefore, are to be the first to hear the text on which they are to preach, they are to practice *lectio divina*, and to recognize the implications of those texts for their own lives, not simply for the lives of others (EG 147–53). With the homily, as with all other aspects of Pope Francis's approach to ministry, the conversion of the minister is the *sine qua non* of fruitful ministry.

CONCLUSION

Pope Francis's interpretation of ministry embodies his passionate desire for the church to be present in history as a body committed to revealing God's mercy. As depicted by the pope, ministers are to be people who hold open the doors of God's mercy, who accompany those in need of that mercy, and who never tire of reminding others that God's mercy is without limit. In order to fulfill those roles authentically, ministers must recognize their own need for mercy; they must understand that they are ministers of mercy rather than owners whose primary task is to preserve a prized possession by protecting it from those they deem unworthy of it. Above all, ministers must be attentive to their relationship with Jesus Christ, the relationship that alone can ensure they do not become self-serving or succumb to any or all idols that can tempt them.

Every emphasis expresses a choice that discards other options. Pope Francis's emphasis on the purpose of ministry means that he does not engage with contentious points in the relationship between lay and ordained ministers, with the future of ministry, or with the broader, and certainly thornier, issue of who can be ordained. Those topics will certainly not fade away, nor can they be matters that continue to be absent from open discussion in the church. What is presently unknowable is how Pope Francis might exercise his leadership to help the church at large address such matters, let alone what outcomes might be possible. What can be said with confidence is that whatever steps Pope Francis takes in regard to the future development of the church's ministry, his goal will be to enable the further realization of the church as a community committed to accompanying the movement of God's mercy in the world.

NOTES

1. "Address of Pope Francis to the Parish Priests of the Diocese of Rome," March 6, 2014, http://w2.vatican.va/content/francesco/en/speeches/2014/march/documents/papa-francesco_20140306_clero-diocesi-roma.html.

2. Ibid.

3. Emmanuel Suhard, *Priests Among Men*, trans. L. Bégin et al. (Notre Dame, IN: Fides, 1964), 88. Cardinal Suhard was the Archbishop of Paris from 1940–49; this text was a pastoral letter to the priests of Paris for Easter in 1949.

4. For an analysis of the uses of "ministry" at Vatican II see, Elissa Rinere, "Conciliar and Canonical Applications of 'Ministry' to the Laity," *The Jurist* 47 (1987): 204–27.

5. For an overview of demographics of ministry, see the statistics provided by the Center for Applied Research in the Apostolate, http://cara.georgetown.edu/CARAServices/requested-churchstats.html.

6. See, for example, Edward Hahnenberg, *Theology of Ministry: An Introduction for Lay Ministers* (Collegeville, MN: Liturgical Press, 2014).

7. For the gap between the church's current practice and its theological categories, see Bernard Sesboüé, "Lay Ecclesial Ministers: A Theological Look into the Future," *The Way* 42 (2003): 67.

8. See, for examples, the articles in William Cahoy, ed., *In the Name of the Church: Vocation and Authorization of Lay Ecclesial Ministry* (Collegeville, MN: Liturgical Press, 2012); and Donna Eschenauer and Harold Daly Horell, eds., *Reflections on Renewal: Lay Ecclesial Ministry and the Church* (Collegeville, MN: Michael Glazier, 2011).

9. Emile Pin, "The Priestly Function in Crisis," in *The Identity of the Priest* [*Concilium* 43], ed. Karl Rahner (New York: Paulist Press, 1969), 45.

10. See, for example, *Ecclesiae de Mysterio*, "Some Questions Regarding Collaboration of Nonordained Faithful in Priests' Sacred Ministry," published jointly by eight Vatican dicastries in 1997; the text can be found in *Origins* 27 (1997): 398–410.

11. Kathleen A. Cahalan, "Towards a Fundamental Theology of Ministry," *Worship* 80, no. 2 (March 2006): 104.

12. Pope Francis, "We Are All Ostiaries," morning meditation, May 12, 2014, http://m.vatican.va/content/francesco/en/cotidie/2014/documents/papa-francesco-cotidie_20140512_ostiaries.html.

13. "Address of Pope Francis to the Parish Priests of the Diocese of Rome," March 6, 2014.

14. Ibid.

15. "Homily of Pope Francis, Ordination Mass in St Peter's Basilica," May 11, 2014, http://w2.vatican.va/content/francesco/en/homilies/2014/documents/papa-francesco_20140511_omelia-ordinazioni-presbiterali.html.

16. Pope Francis, "Homily at the Mass of Chrism," March 28, 2013, http://w2.vatican.va/content/francesco/en/homilies/2013/documents/papa-francesco_20130328_messa-crismale.html.

17. Pope Francis, "Address of Pope Francis to the Parish Priests of the Diocese of Rome," March 6, 2014.

18. Pope Francis, "Homily at the Mass of Chrism," March 28, 2013.

19. Ibid.

20. Pope Francis, "Homily at the Mass of Chrism," April 17, 2014, http://w2.vatican.va/content/francesco/en/homilies/2014/documents/papa-francesco_20140417_omelia-crisma.html.

21. Pope Francis, "What a Priest Should Be," daily meditation, January 11, 2014, http://w2.vatican.va/content/francesco/en/cotidie/2014/documents/papa-francesco-cotidie_20140111_priest.html.

22. Pope Francis, "Sisters and Priests Free from Idolatry," daily meditation, March 3, 2014, http://w2.vatican.va/content/francesco/en/cotidie/2014/documents/papa-francesco-cotidie_20140303_sisters-and-priests.html.

23. Pope Francis, "Homily at a Mass for the Survivors of Clerical Sexual Abuse," July 7, 2014, http://w2.vatican.va/content/francesco/en/cotidie/2014/documents/papa-francesco-cotidie_20140707_vittime-abusi.html.

24. Pope Francis, "Address to the Roman Curia," December 22, 2014, http://w2.vatican.va/content/francesco/en/speeches/2014/december/documents/papa-francesco_20141222_curia-romana.html.

25. Pope Francis, "Address to the Plenary of the Congregation for Clergy," October 3, 2014, http://w2.vatican.va/content/francesco/en/speeches/2014/october/documents/papa-francesco_20141003_plenaria-congregazione-clero.html.

26. Ibid.

27. Pope Francis, "Homily at the Mass of Chrism," April 17, 2014.

28. Pope Francis, "Address to the Roman Curia," December 22, 2014.

CHAPTER 10

THE CHURCH AND SOCIAL JUSTICE

Christine Firer Hinze

When he was elected pope in March 2013, Jorge Bergoglio, SJ, became heir to over a century of official papal statements addressing modern economic, civic, political, and cultural institutions and their impacts on the well-being of persons and communities. This modern "Catholic social teaching" began with Pope Leo XIII's 1891 encyclical on the condition of the working classes through to the present and included Benedict XVI's 2009 analysis of globalized economies in light of the "charity in truth" that human nature and the Christian gospel disclose as essential to justice and peace.[1] Catholic social teaching also comprises episcopal writings, among them the document issued by the regional conference of Latin American bishops (CELAM) following their 2007 meeting in Aparecida, Brazil, in which then Cardinal Bergoglio had a major hand.[2] Rooted in Scripture, Catholic thought and practice, long centuries of Christians' charitable and social action, and dialogue with scholars and activists, Catholic social teaching endeavors to give effective public voice to the church's concern for the dignity and well-being of persons and communities in contemporary cultural, political, economic, and social circumstances.

CATHOLIC SOCIAL TEACHING: KEY THEMES

Across the dramatic historical changes of the past century and a quarter, and amid varieties in focus, occasion, and tone, a recurring set of themes has helped give Catholic social teaching a recognizable public voice.[3] In the eyes of this tradition, social institutions (familial, political, economic, civic) exist to honor, promote, and protect the God-given dignity and value of each and every member. Personal dignity is secured and expressed within communities, whose interdependent members participate in a multi-associational, common good.[4] Solidarity, a practice essential to the common good, describes a *fact* to be acknowledged: the existence of complex interdependencies among persons and communities; a *moral virtue* to be cultivated: dispositions and practices that take up the responsibilities to the common good that these interdependencies imply; and a *Christian virtue* whereby the love of God prompts free, loving self-gift for the good of the neighbors with whom one is linked.[5]

Among social institutions, Catholic social teaching regards the economy's purpose as inclusive provisioning. God intends the fruits of creation for everyone's sustenance, and the fundamental purposes of property, economy, and markets are to make material sustenance—a decent livelihood for self and family—accessible to all, primarily through work that expresses human dignity and creativity, and that serves communities.[6] From this perspective, both unfettered economic liberalism and communistic socialism are based on flawed understandings of humanity and society, and fall short of political economy's aim: to serve and ensure the well-being and integral social development of all members.

Social justice exists when members of society are recognized and treated with dignity, when all receive what is their due, and when every member is able to *participate*—contributing and benefiting—in a vibrant, diverse, common good. Communities are diminished and justice is thwarted when social institutions or their members subordinate pursuit of the common good to the pursuit of partial goods like wealth, power, or status. Recent Catholic social teaching names the maleficent social dynamics and patterns that result as "social sin" or "structures of sin."[7]

To recognize sinful structures, to alleviate the suffering they inflict, and to resist and transform them requires people and communities who enact solidarity—the generous, abiding dedication to the common good of each and all.[8] And to clarify and correct our easily biased visions of what the common good requires, practitioners of solidarity must approach every social circumstance by putting the situations, needs, and aspirations of poor and marginalized persons at the center; that is, through the lens of a preferential option for the poor and vulnerable. "The measure of the greatness of a society is found in the way it treats those most in need, those who have nothing apart from their poverty!"[9] Habitually prioritizing the poor and excluded, asking how social actions, policies, or institutions affect or serve them, helps Christians and their fellow citizens to advance Catholic social teaching's bedrock priority: to promote and protect the value and dignity of each and every human being, within their specific communities and circumstances.

FRANCIS AND SOCIAL JUSTICE

These themes of Catholic social teaching reverberate through Pope Francis's treatment of social justice, but in shapes, tones, and accents that are specifically his own. Francis brings a unique background to his role as spokesperson-in-chief for the church's social justice mission. The Argentinian son of Italian immigrants, Jorge Bergoglio is a broadly educated Jesuit, a former seminary professor who navigated provincial leadership during greatly troubled political times in Argentina,[10] a strong episcopal leader who seemed most at home in the working class and poor communities of Buenos Aires, and a prayerful ascetic who spurns clerical pomp and privilege, preferring to live simply and in close proximity to the ordinary, "faithful people of God."[11] Francis's warm and unassuming persona, his gift for connecting through simple but powerful gestures, his predilection for spontaneous and authentic expressions of piety, enjoyment, and care for people, and a communication style marked by honesty and accessibility, homey expressions and memorable images, all leave audiences and the media alternately delighted and challenged. Many of Francis's social statements have struck observers as fresh, unexpected, even unprecedented. Yet he repeats Catholic social teaching's major tropes, cites his predecessors' social teachings extensively, and recommends that Catholics consult the *Compendium of the Social Doctrine of the Church*.[12] Why, then, do listeners both inside and outside the church find what Francis says about poverty, economy, politics, and justice new or startling, and why does his social rhetoric elicit such strong, sometimes contradictory, responses?

JUSTICE FROM THE HEART

One answer may lie in Francis's capacity to embody and express a religiously grounded vision of social justice that speaks from, and to, the heart. Francis invites Christians to reflect on social justice as he does: from the heart of an intimate relationship with God in Jesus, from the heart of the gospel and the Catholic social tradition, and from the heart of solidarity that "walks Catholic social teaching talk" with and for the poor, the excluded, and the vulnerable. It is on the peripheries of worldly power, Francis proposes, that seekers discover what is truly at the heart of life. Here, among the supposed nobodies and losers of the world, Christians are invited to see, to learn from, and to touch and be touched by the agonized face and suffering body of Jesus in today's world. Francis's profoundly incarnational (spiritual and enfleshed) perspective grounds a perspective on social justice that is the opposite of the abstract, clinical, or formulaic. What comes through is a gospel-rooted, visceral passion for justice that strikes at the heart: both the heart of the message conveyed and the hearts of audiences who receive that message.

AN IGNATIAN CHARACTER

Steeped in Jesuit spirituality and practice, Francis infuses a sense of the church's social mission with a distinctly Ignatian flavor.

In particular, Francis's approach to justice reflects the double movement that Pope Benedict and recent Jesuit congregations cite as a gift and charism of the Society of Jesus: to abide deeply at the heart of the church and to work at the frontiers of faith, culture, and the issues of the day, constantly seeking the most effective ways to share the good news at the most challenging peripheries.[13] Wary of a sociological reduction of the gospel message to an NGO-like social improvement project, Francis's justice rhetoric draws on the prophetic and transformative energies that accompany the gospel's proclamation of Jesus and of God's kingdom.[14] Christians, he tirelessly asserts, are invited to a spiritual life that plunges them deeply into the merciful love of God in Jesus. Anchored in the divine heart, believers are impelled outward to witness to God's inclusive love and merciful compassion "to the ends of the earth." In 2007, then-Cardinal Bergoglio invoked this dual movement in an interview discussing the Latin American bishops' meeting at Aparecida, Brazil. Praying, dialoguing, and writing documents, he emphasized, "isn't sufficient to itself… because the final opening is to the mission.…To abide deeply in the gospel simultaneously impels outward movement" into the places where God's love and justice are most sorely needed. "That is the heart of the mission. Staying, remaining faithful implies an outgoing. Precisely if one remains in the Lord one goes out of oneself."[15]

JUSTICE AS GOD'S MERCY

This pope, who often describes himself as "a sinner,"[16] preaches the church's mission to justice from his fervent conviction that God's *justice as mercy* is core to Christian life. As sinners and pilgrims on life's way, Christians' understanding of justice originates in healing and transforming encounters that reveal God's justice as the outpouring of unmerited, divine mercy (Latin, *misericordia* or "tenderheartedness"; Hebrew, *hesed*, "loving kindness") embodied in Jesus. Like the good shepherd or the father of the prodigal son, God's response to our human failings reveals justice as something much more than following commands or punishing transgressions. Trusting and abiding in God's faithful "mercy-ing" fosters realism and humility in one's relationship to oneself, to one's neighbors, and to God. From hearts connected to God's heart flow gratitude, energies for compassionate solidarity with suffering neighbors, and ardor for justice that impels struggles for structural change.

SPIRIT-ATTUNED AND ANTI-IDEOLOGICAL

Pope Francis enjoins Christians to pursue justice with urgency, but also with humility, flexibility, and attentive receptivity to the promptings of the Holy Spirit who is "a God of surprises." Francis, who himself aspires to this way of proceeding, invokes ancient theologians' depiction of the soul as "a kind of sailing boat," while "the Holy Spirit is the wind that blows in the sail, to send it on its way," and "the impulses and the force of the wind are the gifts of the Spirit. Without His drive, without His grace, we don't go ahead."[17] These Ignatian commitments to spiritual attunement and to adaptability for mission help explain Francis's frequently expressed animus against "ideology." Francis defines ideology as a way of thinking that mistakes partial truths or values for ultimate and complete truth and value. Ideological thinking funds narrow-minded attitudes and actions, whose self-assured and incurious rigidity lead to corrupted systems, and often to great violence and harm. So understood, ideology of any sort—be it market ideology, gender ideology,[18] consumerist ideology, ideological faith,[19] or the ideological colonization of cultures[20]—by totalizing what is partial, tends toward idolatry, and breeds power that is apt to become demonic.[21] By contrast, Christians need to navigate their justice-seeking with a firm but light hand on the rudder, certainly employing maps, but prayerfully attentive to the signs of the times, and poised to follow where the winds of the Spirit might lead.[22]

THREE BASE-POINTS

Francis's evangelical focus and his passionate advocacy for those whom society excludes, exploits, or discards suffuse his reading of the church's social mission, leading him to highlight three related convictions. First, *incarnational solidarity* is a gospel mandate that no Christian may sidestep. Second, *to serve people and to assure conditions for their flourishing* is the central purpose of every social institution. Third, *dignified participation and provisioning* is the decisive standard by which the modern political economies must be judged. Behind his wide-ranging, at times sharply critical, statements on social issues from inequality to immigration, from financial markets to family, this interlinked triad is consistently at work. For Francis, these three tenets do not simply express religious values or aspirational ideals. They affirm realities—what is in fact the case about people and society, and therefore offer justice-seekers a true and reliable orientation for action. It is worth dwelling briefly on each of Francis's signature base-points.

1. INCARNATIONAL SOLIDARITY WITH THE POOR AND VULNERABLE

The gospel, Francis insists, mandates that the church and every Christian draw near to, connect with, and accompany their neighbors in practical, embodied ways—particularly neighbors who are suffering or marginalized, those whom society excludes, exploits, or views as worthless or expendable, those who are vulnerable and lack political or economic power or standing (EG 201).[23] Solidarity that takes action is a religious calling from which no believer or faith community is exempt: "Each individual Christian and every community is called to be an instrument of God for the liberation and promotion of the poor" (EG 187).[24] "God shows the poor 'his first mercy.' This divine preference has consequences for the faith life of all Christians....This is why I want a Church which is poor and for the poor. They have much to teach us" (EG 198). "We may not always be able to reflect adequately the beauty of the Gospel, but there is one sign which we should never lack: the option for those who are least, those whom society discards" (EG 195).

"We incarnate the duty of hearing the cry of the poor when we are deeply moved by the suffering of others." For Francis, solidarity entails contact that is born of tenderhearted compassion (mercy, *hesed*), and that deepens it (EG 93). "Poverty is the flesh of the poor Jesus, in that child who is hungry, in the one who is sick, in those unjust social structures."[25] In Jesus, God inhabits our human lot, taking on our very flesh; disciples of Jesus must practice solidarity not only in thought or word, but in embodied relationships and concrete deeds.

Solidarity means not just assisting from a safe distance, but having "skin in the game" with suffering neighbors, communities, classes, and nations. "It is essential to draw near to new forms of poverty and vulnerability, in which we are called to recognize the suffering Christ, even if this appears to bring us no tangible and immediate benefits." Doing so is a necessary step toward reinstating poor and excluded persons to their rightful status as valued, participating community members. Francis recognizes that for members of individualist, consumerist culture, the prospect of such flesh-to-flesh and heart-to-heart solidarity can be frightening. He offers the following pastoral encouragement:

> Sometimes we are tempted to be that kind of Christian who keeps the Lord's wounds at arm's length. Yet Jesus wants us to touch human misery, to touch the suffering flesh of others. He hopes that we will stop looking for those personal or communal niches which shelter us from the maelstrom of human misfortune and instead enter into the reality of other people's lives and know the power of tenderness. Whenever we do so, our lives become wonderfully complicated and we experience

intensely what it is to be a people, to be part of a people. (EG 270)

Practicing solidarity restores us to reality. It helps treat the "anesthesia of the heart," and releases us from the numbing "soap bubbles of indifference" that our dominant culture fosters.[26] Abiding "at the heart of the people" helps me to discover my authentic self, my heart of flesh.[27] And in so doing, I awaken to my place among the community of other solidary souls: "All around us we begin to see nurses with soul, teachers with soul, politicians with soul, people who have chosen deep down to be with others and for others." Solidarity is thus at the heart of the mission and identity of individual Christians; it is also at the heart of the mission and identity of the church.[28]

Solidarity as a habituated disposition—a social virtue—provides the moral and spiritual infrastructure for long-haul efforts to resist and overcome patterns of injustice. "It presumes the creation of a new mindset which thinks in terms of community and the priority of the life of all over the appropriation of goods by a few" (EG 188–89).[29] When put into practice, these "convictions and habits of solidarity" pave the way for and can help effect needed structural transformations. In the struggle for justice, people converted to solidarity are not simply helpful: they are the indispensable precondition. "Changing structures without generating new convictions and attitudes will only ensure that those same structures will become, sooner or later, corrupt, oppressive and ineffectual" (EG 189).

2. INSTITUTIONS TO SERVE PEOPLE AND TO ASSURE CONDITIONS FOR THEIR FLOURISHING

Social institutions are not abstract mechanisms, but networks of human relations that exist to serve people and their well-being. Properly organized and functioning institutions promote the concrete well-being of each participant, and contribute to conditions that ensure that well-being for all, especially the poor. Viewing social structures and institutions from a perspective informed by solidarity throws their mandate to serve into sharp relief.

Writing to British Prime Minister David Cameron at the opening of the meeting of the G8 in June 2013, Francis underscores this point and the priority of the needs of the poor: "The goal of economics and politics is to serve humanity, beginning with the poorest and most vulnerable wherever they may be, even in their mothers' wombs." In a global economy, "every economic and political theory or action" must be oriented to this fundamental aim: "providing each inhabitant of the planet with the minimum wherewithal to live in dignity and freedom, with the possibility of supporting a family, educating children, praising God and developing one's own human potential."[30]

"The goal of economics and politics is to serve humanity." In so stating, Francis and the Catholic social tradition are doing more than gesturing to an ideal; they are making a claim of fact. On this view, serving all members is constitutive to the adequate functioning of a *polis* or an economy in the same way that the capacity to cut is constitutive to the adequate functioning of a knife. And, like a knife that doesn't cut, an institution that doesn't serve its members is faulty, and must be repaired or replaced. This Catholic viewpoint underlies both what Francis says about contemporary institutions and the sharpness with which he says it. So, in *Evangelii gaudium*, he contends, "Just as the commandment 'Thou shalt not kill' sets a clear limit in order to safeguard the value of human life, today we also have to say 'thou shalt not' to an economy of exclusion and inequality. Such an economy kills" (EG 53).[31] When economic arrangements exclude some people from even minimal participation, that exclusion offends basic human dignity and breeds illegitimate social inequality. Furthermore, any institution that harbors or tolerates these harmful dynamics betrays its constitutive purpose.

These convictions, along with Francis's suspicion of ideological trust in impersonal market mechanisms, resound in oft-quoted statements like the following:

Some people continue to defend trickle-down theories which assume that economic growth, encouraged by a free market, will inevitably succeed in bringing about greater justice and inclusiveness in the world. This opinion, which has never been confirmed by the facts, expresses a crude and naïve trust in the goodness of those wielding economic power and in the sacralized workings of the prevailing economic system. Meanwhile, the excluded are still waiting. (EG 54)

To ensure institutions that fulfill their purposes, "the various grave economic and political challenges facing today's world require a courageous change of attitude that will restore to the end (the human person) and to the means (economics and politics) their proper place." Also consonant with modern Catholic social teaching is Francis's confidence that reorienting institutions' operations to serve their members will not undermine, but ensure their vitality; indeed, "in a seemingly paradoxical way, free and disinterested solidarity is the key to the smooth functioning of the global economy."[32]

3. THE STANDARD OF DIGNIFIED PARTICIPATION AND PROVISIONING

Against this measure, Francis's assessment of currently dominant global market economics is decidedly mixed. On the one hand, business and a "non-exclusive and equitable" market economy have essential roles to play in providing wide access to participation and material well-being.[33] In an interconnected world economy, governments must collaborate in building an inclusive, international common good.

Economy, as the very word indicates, should be the art of achieving a fitting management of our common home, which is the world as a whole. Each meaningful economic decision made in one part of the world has repercussions everywhere else…what is needed at this juncture of history is a more efficient way of interacting which, with due regard for the sovereignty of each nation, ensures the economic well-being of all countries, not just of a few. (EG 206)

But the persistence of poverty and increasing inequality "undermine the workings of inclusive and participatory democracy." Enormous work is needed to address and overcome "the structural causes of inequality and poverty." Faced with these realities, "an authentic faith always implies a deep desire to change the world."[34]

To accomplish the needed changes "requires more than economic growth, while presupposing such growth: it requires decisions, programs, mechanisms and processes specifically geared to a better distribution of income, the creation of sources of employment and an integral promotion of the poor which goes beyond a simple welfare mentality" (EG 204).

It is not enough to offer someone a sandwich unless it is accompanied by the possibility of learning how to stand on one's own two feet. Charity that leaves the poor person as he is, is not sufficient. True mercy, the mercy God gives to us and teaches us, demands justice, it demands that the poor find the way to be poor no longer.[35]

It means working to eliminate the structural causes of poverty and to promote the integral development of the poor, as well as small daily acts of solidarity in meeting the real needs which we encounter. (EG 188)

As Francis declared in an enthusiastic address to an international meeting of grassroots popular justice movements in October 2014, avoiding "paternalistic welfarism" and recognizing the poor as protagonists in their own struggles for economic justice are of paramount importance:

The poor not only suffer injustice but they also struggle against it! They are not content with empty promises, excuses or alibis. Neither are they waiting with folded arms for the aid of NGOs, welfare plans or solutions that never come...or go in one direction, either to anaesthetize or to domesticate....[36]

Building a world of "lasting peace and justice," the pope continues, requires creating "new ways of participation that...animate local, national and international government structures with that torrent of moral energy that arises from the incorporation of the excluded in the building of a common destiny." At all levels, securing the participation and the concrete well-being of persons, families, and communities must be the goal. "Let us say together from our heart: no family without a dwelling, no rural workers without land, no worker without rights, no person without the dignity that work gives."[37]

CONCLUSION

Austen Ivereigh, papal biographer, observes that in Jorge Bergoglio, the cardinals of the 2013 papal conclave found a "once-in-a-generation combination of two qualities seldom found together: he had the political genius of a charismatic leader and the prophetic holiness of a desert saint."[38] For a papacy that has garnered so much popular and media attention, this sort of depiction has its dangers. The point, after all, is not the person of the Bishop of Rome, but the gospel and mission of which he, with all the faithful, is steward and servant. Francis's vision of the church and his aversions to worldliness and to ideology prohibit the uncritical valorization of either his person or his teaching. Thoughtful and informed critics of Francis's statements concerning the economy and politics, women and gender, marriage and family also play important roles in the dialogical development of the modern Catholic social tradition. Still, Ivereigh's observation sheds light on the uniquely compelling way Pope Francis communicates and embodies the heart of the church's social mission, as the ardent pursuit of greater justice for all through compassionate, concrete, and collaborative solidarity with the poor and vulnerable. This solidarity, animated by God's own merciful solidarity with each of us, is crucial to the urgent work of building communities and institutions that serve the dignity and flourishing of each of God's beloved children, and all of us together.

NOTES

1. On modern Catholic social teaching, see, for example, Kenneth J. Himes et al., *Modern Catholic Social Teaching: Commentaries and Interpretations* (Washington, DC: Georgetown University Press, 2005); Donal Dorr, *Option for the Poor and for the Earth: Catholic Social Teaching*, 20th anniv. ed. (Maryknoll, NY: Orbis, 2012); Marvin Krier Mich, *Catholic Social Teaching and Movements* (Mystic, CT: Twenty-Third Publications, 1998); Charles E. Curran, *Catholic Social Teaching: 1891 to Present* (Washington, DC: Georgetown University Press, 2002); *Compendium of the Social Doctrine of the Church* (Vatican City: Liberia Editrice Vaticana, 2004).

2. Bishops of Latin America and the Caribbean, "Concluding Document," Aparecida, Brazil, 2007, http://www.celam.org/aparecida/Ingles.pdf.

3. On the coherence of papal social teaching, cf. Michael Schuck, *That They Be One: The Social Teaching of Papal Encyclicals 1740–1989* (Washington, DC: Georgetown University Press, 1991).

4. Modern Catholic social teaching conceives of flourishing societies as composed of a variety of interdependent groups and associations. A principle of subsidiarity favors widely distributing social power and agency at more local levels, with central authority providing help and support (*subsidium*) to enable smaller units to perform their roles. On this view, the purpose of government is never to dominate or absorb its varied constituencies, but to serve the good of the whole community by providing and overseeing publicly shared goods and activities that more local sectors can-

not and, when needed, by helping other sectors function and contribute according to their particular purposes. Cf. Pope Pius XI, *Quadragesimo anno* (1931), no. 80; *Compendium of the Social Doctrine of the Church*, nos. 185–88.

5. See Pope Paul VI, *Populorum progressio* (1967), no. 48; Pope John Paul II, *Sollicitudo rei socialis* (1987), nos. 26; 36–39; Matthew Lamb, "Solidarity," in Judith Dwyer, ed., *New Dictionary of Catholic Social Thought* (Collegeville, MN: Liturgical Press, 1994), 908–12.

6. "We must never forget that the planet belongs to all mankind and is meant for all mankind; the mere fact that some people are born in places with fewer resources or less development does not justify the fact that they are living with less dignity....We need to grow in a solidarity which 'would allow all peoples to become the artisans of their destiny,' since 'every person is called to self-fulfillment.'" Pope Francis, *Evangelii gaudium*, Apostolic Exhortation, November 24, 2013, no. 190.

7. "Just as goodness tends to spread, the toleration of evil, which is injustice, tends to expand its baneful influence and quietly to undermine any political and social system, no matter how solid it may appear. If every action has its consequences, an evil embedded in the structures of a society has a constant potential for disintegration and death. It is evil crystallized in unjust social structures, which cannot be the basis of hope for a better future." Ibid., no. 59.

8. See Pope John Paul II, *Sollicitudo rei socialis*, no. 37.

9. Catherine Harmon, "Full Text: Pope Francis Visits Rio Shantytown," *Catholic World Report*, July 25, 2013, http://www.catholicworldreport.com/Blog/2446/full_text_pope_francis_visits_rio_shanty_town.aspx.

10. A number of recent biographical accounts of Jorge Bergoglio, SJ, cover this period. Especially comprehensive is Austen Ivereigh, *The Great Reformer: Francis and the Making of a Radical Pope* (New York: Henry Holt, 2014). Cf. also Ross Douthat, "Will Pope Francis Break the Church?" *Atlantic* (May 2015), http://www.theatlantic.com/magazine/archive/2015/05/will-pope-francis-break-the-church/389516/.

11. Ivereigh traces Bergoglio/Francis's developing emphasis on "God's holy, faithful people" in *The Great Reformer*. Even this pope's daily habits—rising at 4 a.m. to pray and reflect, celebrating Mass at 7 a.m., followed by a full schedule of meetings, writing, speaking, and pastoral engagements, all framed by spare, communally oriented patterns of lodging, dining, and dress—bespeak the evangelically focused, contemplative-active rhythm that grounds his social justice teaching and ministry.

12. Ivereigh remarks that Francis's statements on the economy in *Evangelii gaudium* were among the least original in the text. In line with modern papal teaching, "Francis wasn't critiquing the market in the sense of the free exchange of goods and services and ordinary human economic activity…even less was he proposing a collectivist or any other alternative 'system.' He was unmasking an idolatrous mindset that had surrendered human sovereignty to a hidden deity, a *deus ex machina*, which demanded to be left alone to function unimpeded. What Francis deplored were ideologies that defend the absolute autonomy of the marketplace." Ibid., 213.

13. Society of Jesus, General Congregation 35, decree no. 3: "To be missioned to this work at the new frontiers of our times always requires that we also be rooted at the very heart of the Church. This tension, specific to the Ignatian charism, opens the way to true creative fidelity." Cf. Pope Benedict, "Address to the Fathers of the General Congregation of the Society of Jesus," February 21, 2008, http://w2.vatican.va/content/benedict-xvi/en/speeches/2008/february/documents/hf_ben-xvi_spe_20080221_gesuiti.html.

14. Cf. Pope Francis, Homily, "Missa Pro Ecclesia" with the Cardinal Electors (March 14, 2013), http://www.vatican.va/holy_father/francesco/homilies/2013/documents/papa-frances co_20130314_omelia-cardinali_en.html.

15. "What I would have said at the Consistory: An interview with Cardinal Jorge Mario Bergoglio," Archbishop of Buenos Aires by Sefania Falasca, *30 Giorni* (Italy), November 2011.

16. Antonio Spadaro, SJ, "A Big Heart Open to God," exclusive interview with Pope Francis, *America*, September 30, 2013, http://americamagazine.org/pope-interview.

17. Falasca, "What I Would Have Said at the Consistory."

18. On gender ideology, see Pope Benedict XVI, "Christmas Address to the Roman Curia," December 2, 2012, http://w2.vati can.va/content/benedict-xvi/en/speeches/2012/december/docu ments/hf_ben-xvi_spe_20121221_auguri-curia.html; cf. also Joshua McElwee, "Francis Strongly Criticizes Gender Theory, Comparing it to Nuclear Arms," *National Catholic Reporter*, February 13, 2013, http://ncronline.org/news/vatican/francis-strongly-criticizes-gender-theory-comparing-nuclear-arms.

19. See Pope Francis, "Address to the Leadership of the Episcopal Conferences of Latin America," World Youth Day Coordination Meeting, Rio de Janeiro, Brazil, July 28, 2013, section 4, http://w2.vatican.va/content/francesco/en/speeches/2013/july/documents/papa-francesco_20130728_gmg-celam-rio.html.

20. See Alan Holdren, "Pope Francis Warns West Over 'Ideological Colonization,'" *National Catholic Register*, January 20, 2015, http://www.ncregister.com/daily-news/pope-francis-warns-west-over-ideological-colonization.

21. See Francis's treatment of the "new idolatry of money," *Evangelii gaudium*, nos. 55–56.

22. "We need to invoke the Spirit constantly....It is true that this trust in the unseen can cause us to feel disoriented....I myself have frequently experienced this. Yet there is no greater freedom than that of allowing oneself to be guided by the Holy Spirit, renouncing the attempt to plan and control everything to the last detail, and instead letting him enlighten, guide and direct us, leading us wherever he wills" (*Evangelii gaudium* 280). This sensibility affects Francis's perspective on history: "God manifests himself in time and is present in the processes of history. This gives priority to actions that give birth to new historical dynamics. And it requires patience, waiting." Spadaro, "A Big Heart Open to God."

23. Cf. also Ivereigh, *The Great Reformer*, 211: "*Evangelii gaudium* is redolent with the themes of Aparecida 2007," including, "A Church of and for the poor, rooted in the Second Vatican Council, geared to mission, focused on the margins, centered on God's holy faithful people, in confident dialogue with culture yet bold in denouncing what harmed the poor."

24. Cf. also ibid., no. 201: "None of us can think we are exempt from concerns for the poor and for social justice."

25. Pope Francis, "Address to the Students of the Jesuit Schools of Italy and Albania," June 7, 2013, https://w2.vatican.va/content/francesco/en/speeches/2013/june/documents/papa-francesco_20130607_scuole-gesuiti.html. See also, *Evangelii gaudium* 210.

26. "The Pope on Lampedusa: 'The Globalization of Indifference,'" *Vatican News*, July 8, 2013, http://www.news.va/en/news/pope-on-lampedusa-the-globalization-of-indifferenc.

27. "My mission of being at the heart of the people is not just a part of my life or a badge I can take off: it is not an extra or just another moment in life. Instead it is something I cannot uproot from my being without destroying my very self. I am a mission on this earth; that is the reason why I am here in this world. We have to regard ourselves as sealed, even branded by this mission of bringing light, blessing, enlivening, raising up, healing and freeing" (*Evangelii gaudium* 273).

28. "Any Church community, if it thinks it can comfortably go its own way without creative concern and effective cooperation in helping the poor to live with dignity and reaching out to everyone, will also risk breaking down" (Ibid., no. 207).

29. In line with Catholic social teaching, solidary Christians recognize that "the social function of property and the universal destination of goods are realities which come before private property…for this reason, solidarity must be lived as the decision to restore to the poor what belongs to them" (Ibid., no. 149).

30. Pope Francis, "Letter to H.M. Prime Minister David Cameron, on the Opening of the G8 Meeting," June 15–18, 2013," https://w2.vatican.va/content/francesco/en/letters/2013/documents/papa-francesco_20130615_lettera-cameron-g8.html.

31. Cf. also Andrea Tornielli and Giacomo Galeazzi, *This Economy Kills: Pope Francis on Capitalism and Social Justice* (Collegeville, MN: Liturgical Press, 2015).

32. "Letter to Prime Minister David Cameron." This claim that good ethics and good economics go hand in hand, frequently adduced in Catholic social teaching, is reflected in exhortations such as the following: "The need to resolve the structural causes

of poverty cannot be delayed, not only for the pragmatic reason of its urgency for the good order of society, but because society needs to be cured of a sickness which is weakening and frustrating it, and which can only lead to new crises" (*Evangelii gaudium* 202).

33. "Business is a vocation, and a noble vocation, provided that those engaged in it see themselves challenged by a greater meaning in life; this will enable them truly to serve the common good by striving to increase the goods of this world and to make them more accessible to all" (Ibid., no. 203). Moving toward a more just global economy "requires, on one hand, significant *reforms* that provide for the redistribution of the wealth produced and universalization of free markets at the service of families, and, on the other, the redistribution of sovereignty, on both the national and supranational planes." Pope Francis, "Address to Participants in the Plenary of the Pontifical Council for Justice and Peace," October 2, 2014, https://w2.vatican.va/content/francesco/en/speeches/2014/october/documents/papa-francesco_20141002_pont-consiglio-giustizia-e-pace.html.

34. Pope Francis, "Homily on the Memorial of the Most Holy Name of Jesus," Church of the Gesu, Rome, January 3, 2014, https://w2.vatican.va/content/francesco/en/homilies/2014/documents/papa-francesco_20140103_omelia-santissimo-nome-gesu.html.

35. Pope Francis, "Address: Visit to the Jesuit Refugee Service in Rome," September, 10, 2013, https://w2.vatican.va/content/francesco/en/speeches/2013/september/documents/papa-francesco_20130910_centro-astalli.html.

36. Pope Francis, "The Pope's Address to Popular Movements," Vatican City, *Zenit*, October, 29, 2014, http://www.zenit.org/en/articles/pope-s-address-to-popular-movements.

37. Echoing previous papal social encyclicals, Francis stresses that the right to employment "cannot be considered a variable dependent on financial and monetary markets." Decent employment "is a fundamental good in regard to dignity, to the formation of a family, to the realization of the common good and of peace." These three, "Education, work and access to health care for all…are key elements for development and the

just distribution of goods, for the attainment of social justice, for membership in society...and for free and responsible participation in political life." Pope Francis, "Address to Plenary of Pontifical Council of Justice and Peace," October 2, 2014.

38. Ivereigh, *The Great Reformer*, 357.

CONCLUSION

Richard R. Gaillardetz

What are we to make of this new pontificate? Even in the pages of this volume, there are notably different portraits of our first Jesuit pope and first pope from the Global South. Imbelli has argued for a deep continuity between Pope Francis and Pope Benedict on the basis of a shared Christocentrism and commitment to the new evangelization. He is right to do so. Mannion notes Francis's decisive move away from Benedict's restrictive version of a *communio*-ecclesiology and toward a recovery of the Council's teaching on the church as the new people of God. He is also right to do so.

The papacy is a two-thousand-year–old ecclesiastical institution profoundly shaped by longstanding rituals and customs and committed to preserving the fidelity of the apostolic faith from age to age—within the history of such an institution, profound continuity is a given. Yet popes of any significance, given enough time, have found ways to leave their distinctive stamp on both the papacy and the church. The language of continuity versus discontinuity doesn't really do justice to what our church is experiencing in the present Bishop of Rome. The limits of this kind of language are nowhere more evident than when we consider Pope Francis in the light of the Second Vatican Council, the most important event in the history of modern Catholicism.

The legacy of each of his five immediate predecessors will, in some sense, all be tied to that Council. Pope John, of course, gave us a new, pastoral vision for the church and dared to imagine the possibilities for convening the first ecumenical council in almost a century. Yet he died after the Council's first session when many of the most influential documents were only in a germinal stage. Pope Paul VI presided over the final three sessions. Although he was prone to frequent intrusions in the conciliar process, without his determination to stay the conciliar course, many of the more contentious Council documents would not have been promulgated. In the wake of the Council, he advanced the church's social teaching, encouraged the implementation of the Council's liturgical reform, created an international theological commission, and internationalized the Curia. Yet he also ignored the Council's call for more robust institutional expressions of episcopal collegiality and backed away from the recommendations of a commission he reconstituted (after its initial creation by Pope John XIII) to revisit the church's prohibition of artificial birth control.

Even the brief pontificate of John Paul I was an affirmation of the conciliar legacy, as evident in his choice of papal name. Karol Wojtyla was himself an influential bishop at the Council. As John Paul II, his pontificate advanced the Council's commitment to engage the modern world, even if that engagement was interpreted through the lens of his Polish experience of the Cold War. No pope has done more to further Jewish-Christian relations and to effect a rapprochement between science and religion. His frequent travels heightened our sense of the global character of the church, and his groundbreaking meetings in Assisi to pray with the leaders of various world religions enfleshed the Council's call for a more positive interreligious dialogue. Yet his bold engagement with the world was matched by an indifference to the mechanics of ecclesial governance, disappointing episcopal appointments, and a rigid intolerance of internal dissent.

Pope Benedict XVI can also lay claim to the Council, having contributed to it directly as an influential *peritus*. His considerable theological contributions furthered select trajectories in conciliar teaching. Still, his tenure as prefect of the CDF and his eight-year pontificate advanced a program to ward off all but the most cautious interpretations of Council teaching. In the end, his conciliar legacy may be tarnished by his resistance to much of the Council's far-ranging liturgical reform. Ironically, his greatest contribution to the church as pope may have been his resignation from papal office, representing as it did a desacralization of the papacy.

Although he was not ordained a priest until years after the Council, Pope Francis stands within the legacy of the Council. Indeed, the chapters in this volume make a persuasive case that his pontificate represents the most ambitious and comprehensive effort of the postconciliar papacy to bring to life the reforming vision of the Council. Clifford highlights the extent to which the priority of dialogue, evident on almost every page of conciliar text, informs Pope Francis's view of the church. Rausch sees in Francis a determination to tease out the implications of the Second Vatican Council's teaching that the revelation of God constituted the people of God as a listening church. Ruddy perceptively explores how Pope Francis has continued what Joseph Komonchak once called the "Copernican revolution" of Vatican II, its rediscovery of a theology of the local church. Francis sees the relationship between the local churches and the universal church in the light of his call to move from the center to the peripheries. Lennan notes how Francis has eschewed the postconciliar hand-wringing regarding ministerial identity to recover the Council's insistence on a more pastorally oriented view of ministry in which all called to ministry, ordained and lay, must be willing to accompany the people on their journey through life.

The Second Vatican Council taught that the church was "missionary by its very nature." This could well stand as the leitmotif of Francis's pontificate. According to Bingemer, Francis has called all the baptized to abandon the security of our easy certitudes and ecclesiastical refuges in order to "go into the streets" to meet the broken and wounded of the world. González-Andrieu locates Francis's commitment to mission in his sensitivity to the demand for an inculturated faith and an appreciation for the deep aesthetic vitality of popular religion. Firer Hinze demonstrates how Francis is motivated by a vision of social justice "that speaks from, and to, the heart." Gaillardetz argues that the church's mission provides the necessary context for any pastorally attuned appropriation of church teaching.

History may well look back on the pontificate of Francis as that decisive moment in the history of the church in which the full force of the Second Vatican Council's reformist vision was finally realized. If so, then fifty years from now, the conversation about Pope Francis may not be about the extent of his continuity with his predecessors. In 2065, on the hundredth anniversary of Vatican II, church historians may instead be measuring the popes who succeed Francis by their fidelity to *his* legacy as the preeminent pope of the Council.

CONTRIBUTORS

Maria Clara Bingemer (PhD, Gregorian University, Rome) is full professor at the Theology Department of the Catholic University of Rio de Janeiro (PUC-Rio). She teaches fundamental theology and theology of God. She is also on the editorial board of *Concilium*. Widely published in many languages in those areas and also in spirituality and mysticism, recent books in English include the following: *A Face for God* (Convivium) and with P. Casarella, ed. *Witnessing: Prophecy, Politics, and Wisdom* (Orbis). She has also published many articles in journals such as *Concilium* and *Modern Theology*.

Catherine E. Clifford (PhD, St. Michael's College, Toronto) is professor of systematic and historical theology in the Faculty of Theology, Saint Paul University, Ottawa. Teaching and writing in the areas of ecclesiology, ecumenism, and Vatican II studies, she has recently authored *Decoding Vatican II: Interpretation and Ongoing Reception* (Paulist), *Keys to the Council: Unlocking the Teaching of Vatican II* (with Richard R. Gaillardetz), *The Groupe des Dombes: A Dialogue of Conversion* (Peter Lang), and edited *A Century of Prayer for Christian Unity* and *For the Communion of the Churches*. She is the translator of *One Teacher: Doctrinal Authority in the Church* (all Eerdmans).

Richard R. Gaillardetz (PhD, Notre Dame) is the Joseph Professor of Catholic Systematic Theology at Boston College. He is the author of numerous articles and author or editor of ten books, including *An Unfinished Council: Vatican II, Pope Francis and the Renewal of Catholicism* (Michael Glazier) and *Keys to the Council: Unlocking the Teaching of Vatican II* (with Catherine E. Clifford). From 2013 to 2014, he served as the president of the Catholic Theological Society of America.

Cecilia González-Andrieu (PhD, Graduate Theological Union) is associate professor of theology at Loyola Marymount University in Los Angeles. A bilingual and bicultural scholar, her principal areas of research merge the concerns of Latino/a theology with theological aesthetics and systematic theology. Regarded as one of the leading voices in the development of theological aesthetics in the United States, her publications include *Bridge to Wonder: Art as a Gospel of Beauty* (Baylor), *Teaching Global Theologies: Power and Praxis* (with Pui-Lan Kwok), and articles such as "How Does Beauty Save? Evocations from Federico Garcia Lorca's *Teoria y Juego del Duende*" (*Cithara*).

Christine Firer Hinze (PhD, Chicago) is professor of theological ethics and the director of the Francis & Ann Curran Center for American Catholic Studies at Fordham University. Her teaching and publications focus on Catholic social thought, political and economic ethics, women and families, and the dynamics of structural justice. Her most recent monograph, *Glass Ceilings and Dirt Floors: Women, Work, and the Global Economy* (Paulist), is based on her 2014 Madeleva Lecture.

Robert P. Imbelli (PhD, Yale) is associate professor emeritus of theology at Boston College. A priest of the Archdiocese of New York, he also taught at St. Joseph's Seminary, Dunwoodie, and the Maryknoll School of Theology. He wrote the article "Holy Spirit," for *The New Dictionary of Theology*, edited the volume *Handing On the Faith: The Church's Mission and Challenge* (Crossroad), and recently published *Rekindling the Christic Imagination: Theological Meditations for the New Evangelization* (Liturgical).

Richard Lennan (D. Theol., Innsbruck) is professor of systematic theology in the School of Theology and Ministry at Boston College. He is a priest of the diocese of Maitland-Newcastle (Australia) and a former president of the Australian Catholic Theological Association. His teaching and research focus on ecclesiology, fundamental theology, and the theology of Karl Rahner. He is the author or editor of six books, the latest of which (as co-editor) is *Hope: Promise, Possibility, and Fulfillment* (Paulist).

Gerard Mannion (DPhil, Oxford) holds the Joseph and Winifred Amaturo Chair in Catholic Studies at Georgetown University, where he is also a senior research fellow with the Berkley Center for Religion, Peace and World Affairs and co-director of its Church and World Program. He has published widely in the fields of ecclesiology, ecumenism and in ethics, and serves as chair of the Ecclesiological Investigations International Research Network.

Thomas P. Rausch, SJ, (PhD, Duke) is the T. Marie Chilton Professor at Loyola Marymount University in Los Angeles. Widely published in the areas of Christology, ecclesiology, ecumenism, and contemporary Catholicism, recent books include *Eschatology, Liturgy, and Christology* (Michael Glazier); *This is Our Faith: An Introduction to Catholicism*; and *Faith, Hope, and Charity: Pope Benedict XVI on the Theological Virtues* (both Paulist).

Christopher Ruddy (PhD, Notre Dame) is associate professor of historical and systematic theology at the Catholic University of America in Washington, DC. He specializes in ecclesiology, the history and theology of the Second Vatican Council, and the *nouvelle théologie* and *ressourcement* movements. He is the author of *The Local Church: Tillard and the Future of Catholic Ecclesiology* and *Tested in Every Way: The Catholic Priesthood in Today's Church* (both Herder & Herder), as well as articles in journals such as *Theological Studies* and *The Thomist*.